EXPLORING THE WORLD OF INSECTS

THE EQUINOX GUIDE TO INSECT BEHAVIOUR

ADRIAN FORSYTH

CAMDEN HOUSE

CAMDEN
•HOUSE•
✦✦✦✦✦
PUBLISHING

© Copyright 1992 Adrian Forsyth

Canadian Cataloguing in Publication Data

Forsyth, Adrian
  Exploring the world of insects : the Equinox
guide to insect behaviour

Includes index.
ISBN 0-921820-47-X (bound)   ISBN 0-921820-49-6 (pbk.)

1. Insects − Juvenile literature.   2. Insects.
I. Title.

QL467.2.F67   1992   j595.7   C92-094740-9

Front and back cover photographs by
Robert McCaw

Designed by
Linda J. Menyes

Camden House Publishing
(a division of Telemedia Communications Inc.)
7 Queen Victoria Road
Camden East, Ontario K0K 1J0

Box 766
Buffalo, NY 14240-0766

Colour separations by
Hadwen Graphics
Ottawa, Ontario

Printed and bound in Canada by
Tri-Graphic Printing
Ottawa, Ontario

Printed on acid-free paper

Trade distribution by
Firefly Books
250 Sparks Avenue
Willowdale, Ontario
Canada M2H 2S4

P.O. Box 1325
Ellicott Station
Buffalo, NY 14205

Contents

The Success of Insects

The red-spotted tortoise beetle, above, is a member of the order Coleoptera, the most diverse group of animals on Earth. The group contains 300,000 known species, commonly referred to as beetles. The damselfly, right, has emerged from its nymphal skin. As a nymph, it lived underwater, but it will now spend the rest of its life as a flying predator.

Some of the strangest and most beautiful animals I have ever seen have been insects. On my first visit to the rainforest of western Ecuador, I was sleeping in a room with the window open. In the black of night, I awoke to find the room pulsing with weird moving lights. Pairs of green luminous spots like small eyes blinked on and off, and orange streaks flew through the air only to disappear suddenly. I lay still, watching the lights weave back and forth, flickering on and off, unable to get a better look because there was no electricity.

When the sun rose in the morning, I discovered the source of the peculiar light show. Large click beetles the size of my little finger had flown in through the open window. Each had two green light spots on the midsec-

tion and a bright orange light organ on the underside of the abdomen. Since that time, I have often watched click beetles flying through the nighttime forest, leaving their lovely trails of light. No matter how many times I see this sight, its beauty never fades.

It is virtually impossible to run out of insects to admire and learn about. In fact, most of the animals that walk, fly and burrow about this planet are insects. They dominate Earth not only by their sheer numbers but also by their variety. Roughly 800,000 species have already been scientifically described, and that number represents 80 percent of all known animal species.

Some scientists believe that there are approximately three million different kinds of insects alive today. Others claim that the total number of insect species is closer to 30 million. To try to imagine the scale we are dealing with, consider that there are only about 250,000 kinds of plants on Earth. A single insect family – that of the ants, for instance – contains roughly 10,000 species, more species than there are in the whole bird family. Insect families such as the weevils may have more than 100,000 species. And there are even more beetle species than there are plant species.

The number of individual insects is even more staggering. Scientists estimate that half a hectare of soil in a meadow contains between 400 million and 400 billion individual insects, most of which are tiny springtails and ants.

How should you explore the world

Coloration in insects can serve as an early warning to would-be predators. The brightly coloured stinkbug, right, defends itself from attack with a noxious, offensive secretion.

of insects? Animals are always more interesting when they have a name. For scientists and advanced students of insects, an identification system that classifies and organizes all insects into groups is essential, and beginning an insect collection is an important start to that process.

But this is not a book about identifying and collecting insects. There are already many books that will help you do that. Instead, this is a book about the lives of insects, about figuring out where they live, what they eat and why they do the things they do.

I suggest that you start by using your eyes and ears. It is fun to watch and listen to insects in action, and you can usually identify an insect if you make careful observations of it. It is also useful to become familiar with the basic elements of the insect body plan. Their physical design is the key to understanding why insects are so successful.

Insects lack an internal skeleton. They have no spine, or vertebrae, and are therefore classed as invertebrates. In place of the spine, they have a relatively stiff outer skeleton. This exoskeleton, which is so obvious on a bright, shiny beetle, is highly effective for small organisms because it has all the design advantages of a corrugated tin can or culvert. Lightweight yet strong, the exoskeleton protects the powerful muscles on the inside. The presence of the exoskeleton also explains why some insects are the only invertebrates that have wings – it is light and rigid enough to endure the stresses of flight and helps to give insects streamlined, aerodynamic bodies.

Insects also have three pairs of legs, fewer than other invertebrates. Compare a flying wasp with a common invertebrate such as a spider or a millipede, and you will see how elegantly suited for flight an insect is.

The physical design of insects also allows them to be amazingly strong. An ant can lift and carry 10 times its body weight over its head for long distances. Some beetles are able to lift 800 times their own weight. When I have tried to hold a walnut-sized scarab beetle in my fist, it has dug and pushed its way out from between my closed fingers.

The basic body structure of an insect is fairly simple. Every insect has a head, a thorax region to which its six legs are attached and an abdomen. The way in which these parts differ from species to species tells us a lot. When you examine an insect's head, look at its mouthparts. Are they suited for chewing, as are the beetle's, or does the insect have a long tubular structure, as do bugs that suck fluids? Are their eyes enlarged, like those of predatory dragonflies and night-flying moths, or are they tiny, like the eyes of ants, which use their sense of smell to navigate?

There are many explanations for why insects have been so successful, but the most important is simple: insects are small. Even the largest – the big rhinoceros beetle that fills your hand or tropical moths with wingspans up to 30 centimetres – do not count as large animals. The smallest insects are incredibly minute and could easily fit on the head of a pin. Many wasps are only 0.25 millimetre long. Weighing in at just one microgram each, nearly 500 million of them would be required to tip the scale at half a kilogram. Whenever I watch one of these little wasps crawling along a leaf, I marvel that such a tiny speck can contain a brain, a nervous system connected to muscles and a variety of digestive organs – all the intricate working parts which make up complex animals.

Small size has proved to be an advantage for insects because it enables them to live and feed on resources that are far too minuscule to interest larger animals. There are wasps that feed and grow to maturity within a single butterfly egg; the butterfly itself develops from a caterpillar which lives on a diet of leaves that would be barely a mouthful for a cow.

You could spend your whole life just becoming familiar with the hundreds of different moths and butterflies that live in most areas of North America. Some might ask why anyone would want to do such a thing. But who would not be fascinated by the sight of a monarch butterfly cracking open its green, gold-spotted chrysalis and crawling forth as a magnificent orange-and-black-winged flying machine? On warm summer nights, when I see ghostly green long-tailed luna moths fluttering around my porch lights, I am reminded once again that indeed, some of the strangest and most beautiful animals I have ever seen have been insects.

Camouflage and Mimicry

Many insects have evolved an appearance that enables them to blend into the surrounding vegetation. The thornlike green treehoppers, above, are inconspicuous when sitting motionless on the stems of thorny acacia trees. The tropical caterpillar, right, uses false eyespots and manipulates its body into a wedge-shaped snake head to mimic a venomous viper.

One afternoon while taking a rest during a hike in Costa Rica, I watched a bright yellowish butterfly lazily float by. The butterfly circled back, then settled to the ground a few metres from where I sat. Folding its wings, it suddenly vanished. I strained my eyes in its direction but was unable to see it. Slowly, I inched toward the spot where it had landed. Only when I was within reach of it did I realize that the butterfly was still quietly sitting there. By folding its wings together, it had concealed its brilliant yellow upper wings with the surface of its lower wings, which were a dull, greyish brown. With their pointed tips and network of veins, these wings allowed the butterfly to blend perfectly into the litter of dead leaves.

Every field and forest is constantly patrolled by sharp-eyed birds and animals that eat insects, which makes camouflage a necessary part of almost every insect's defence repertoire. Birds can be especially dangerous predators. Not only do many feed primarily on insects, but they are also able to see colour and to detect more detail than humans can. I was amazed to watch through binoculars as a nuthatch worked its way up the trunk of a maple tree, picking up one tiny insect after another. When I inspected the same tree trunk, I could see scarcely any insects.

In tropical forests, birds are joined by other sharp-eyed animals that eat insects. Many monkeys include insects in their diet, as do lizards and snakes. For edible insects without

any chemical defence or weapons, the best protection against such perceptive predators is camouflage.

Camouflage means the ability to blend into the background. It takes a hunter some time to inspect the bark and twigs and vegetation in a forest. It is not surprising, then, that many insects have brown or grey swirling patterns which blend in with bark or brown leaf litter. The complex markings on the wings of many butterflies and moths make it difficult for a predator to distinguish the outline of the insect from the rest of its environment. This is called "disruptive coloration," because it disrupts the eye's ability to recognize a separate body form.

Other insects conceal themselves by mimicking common inedible objects. I have come upon caterpillars that are almost perfect imitations of bird droppings. Only through accidentally bumping the caterpillars on their leaves and causing them to move did I discover their true identity. Many katydids, butterflies and moths look remarkably like dead leaves, with wings that have false leaf veins, pointed tips and even spots and cutout sections which resemble the decay process. Other insects assume long, skinny, rolled-up postures and make themselves look like twigs and sticks. The sap-sucking insects known as treehoppers feed on plant stems and often resemble thorns.

Caddis flies, which live in streams and ponds, construct a protective case of silk or sand grains held together with sticky secretions. Some even build cases that look exactly like old snail shells. The same sort of woven cocoon is used by psychid moth caterpillars, which carry a case of bark, sand, plant fragments and sticks. As long as the caterpillar remains still, it is almost impossible to know that there is a living animal inside that mass of debris.

Playing dead is an important strategy for camouflaged insects. If you disturb insects such as dull brown plant-eating weevils, they often drop to the ground and lie rigidly. Animals can easily detect movement, so the key to the insect's survival is to remain absolutely motionless until the bird, monkey or lizard has given up and moved on. Many moths that rest on bark and imitate it with their upper wings combine camouflage with this second backup defence. To observe this behaviour, set up an ultraviolet light and hang a white sheet in front of it on a warm, damp night, preferably one that is still and moonless. Attracted by the light, moths will eventually settle on the sheet and, by morning, will be quietly resting to avoid the birds. That will give you a chance to examine their camouflage up close. Notice how conspicuous they are on a white sheet or house wall, but imagine how difficult it would be to spot them on a tree trunk.

Late in the summer, underwing moths are plentiful. If you disturb one of these grey-mottled moths when it is resting by tapping it lightly with your finger, it will suddenly flip its forewings ahead and expose bright red-, orange- or yellow-banded underwings. Then it will probably fly

When at rest on a tree trunk, the large sphinx moth, above right, is camouflaged. Its mottled grey forewings conceal brightly coloured hind wings, allowing the moth to blend into the pattern of the bark. If pecked by a bird, however, the moth will flip up its wings, producing a flash of colour and creating the impression of a face with its eyespots. Often, the suddenness of the moth's display is enough to frighten away the bird. The grey, barklike texture and the angular posture and long limbs of the African praying mantis, far right, simultaneously increase its effectiveness as an ambush-type predator of other insects and enable it to avoid attacks by birds.

away. This flash of colour is known as a "startle display," and its purpose is to surprise birds long enough to allow the moth to escape. The best example of a well-developed startle display is that of the large Io moth. Rather than bands of colour, the Io moth flashes two huge false eyes. Scales on its hind wings look strikingly like a pair of glaring owl eyes. Since most small insect-eating birds are terrified of owls, the startle display is very effective. This tactic is also used by other insects, such as the lanternfly, which has a strange peanut-shaped head, and some praying mantises.

False eyespots, even when not accompanied by a startle display, can be found in many insects, especially butterflies. When a bird sees a butterfly or other insect, it instinctively pecks at the eye and head region as a way to kill its prey quickly. To mislead the bird, butterflies have large false eyespots located on the tips of their wings. If the bird pecks at the false eyespot, it damages only the wing, not the vital head or body. The butterfly is then able to escape. The hairstreak butterfly found in Costa Rica combines false eyes at the tips of its hind wings with two long, wispy filaments that resemble antennae. Perched on a leaf, it slowly wiggles the fake antennae up and down, making it very difficult for a predator to know which end is which.

An insect's startle display can act as a threatening form of mimicry. I was once shocked when casually looking at a flowering bush in Costa Rica by the sudden appearance of a green palm viper in the leaves. What I had done, however, was interfere with a cigar-sized sphinx moth caterpillar. When disturbed, this caterpillar rears up and begins weaving back and forth like a snake. At the same time, it constricts part of its body to create the impression of a neck while flattening the forward sections to resemble a head, complete with two large false eyes. The result is a credible imitation of a snake, a display that must intimidate both birds and monkeys. It fooled me.

Most insect imitations are of other insects. Harmless edible insects often mimic insects that have weapons, such as bees or wasps, or insects that have a powerful chemical defence. I have watched robber flies perching by flowers in such a perfect imitation

of large, hairy bumblebees that I had to net them to determine whether they were flies or bees. They even make the same angry buzzing noise of bumblebees. Since birds avoid bumblebees, which sting powerfully, the robber fly imitators can, in this way, protect themselves. Many other harmless flies and moths and some beetles also have this colour pattern and thereby mislead birds about their identity.

To avoid attack by birds, some insects imitate the appearance of bad-tasting insects. The monarch butterfly, for example, is defended and protected by the poison it collected from milkweed plants while feeding as a caterpillar. The viceroy butterfly has none of these poisons, since its diet is willows and cherries, but it is safe from birds because it is such a good mimic of a monarch. This kind of mimicry is widespread throughout the insect world.

Mimicry and camouflage provide much of the fun of observing insects. They are part of an ecological puzzle that challenges both our eyes and our intellect.

11

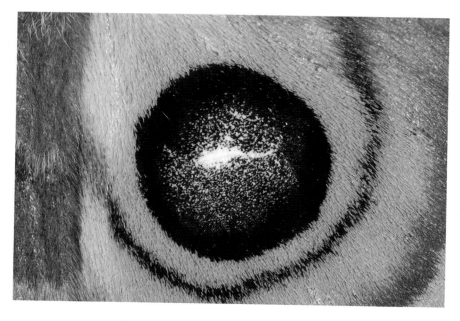

Defence

The scales on the hind wings of the Io moth, above, "paint" a false eye when flashed at a bird that has come too close to the resting moth. When the Chinese praying mantis, right, is threatened, it flares its wings in an aggressive posture that exaggerates its size.

In the tropical rainforest, I usually make it a practice to wear a long-sleeved shirt, even when it is hot. Once, having broken my own rule, I was walking along an overgrown trail wearing just a T-shirt. Suddenly, I felt a fiery sensation running along my forearm. I looked down and saw angry red welts forming on my skin. What had caused them? When I examined the bushes more closely, I saw a mass of beautiful lime-green caterpillars covered with reddish yellow spines. They were so appealing that it was tempting to pick one up. But painful experience has taught me that some of the most handsome species are also the worst insects to handle. Just brushing against those long spines had been like running into stinging nettles.

The caterpillars had a reason for stinging me: it was a clear case of self-defence. Most insects are small and vulnerable to attack by birds, lizards, spiders and other predators. As a result, they have developed many defensive structures and behaviours. Because butterflies and moths are always at risk of flying into spiderwebs, their wings are covered with detachable scales. When these insects are caught in a web or held in the grasp of a predator, the scales pull away freely and thus enable the moth or butterfly to slip away. You will see these scales on your fingertips no matter how gently you handle a moth.

The evasive tactics of some moths can be even more sophisticated. Moths that fly at night are often attacked and eaten by bats, which detect and track the moths using echolocation. The bats emit high-frequency sounds, then listen for echoes that indicate the position and flight path of the moth. Many tiger moths counter this strategy with their own sounds. When a tiger moth hears bat signals or detects the sound of a bat homing in, it stops flying and abruptly drops like a stone while making high-pitched noises. Its signals confuse and distract the bat, which allows the moth to escape.

Some insects use brute force as a defence. If you pick up a large long-horn beetle, a tiger beetle, a dobsonfly or a katydid, you will find it bites persuasively with its long, sharp mandibles. Insects like grasshoppers use powerful hind legs to rocket away from danger. I have had 15-centime-

Smaller than your eyelash, the stinger itself would do little damage. But it acts as a tiny hypodermic needle that injects small, potent amounts of dozens of chemicals, including enzymes and other compounds, which produce pain, swelling and allergic reactions. As many as 50 different chemicals are mixed together in ant, bee and wasp venom.

Many caterpillars have a less active but equally effective stinging defence: they are covered with hairs that irritate the skin with the same chemicals produced by stinging nettles. Barely brushing against one of these bristly caterpillars can raise fiery red welts on your arm, as I discovered. Some of the softest-looking caterpillars – one has the local name "golden guinea pig caterpillar" – sting strongly enough to cause people to faint with pain. Fortunately, these are found mainly in tropical forests and are not common.

Insects without stingers or strong mouthparts can often deter attackers with a toxic spray. The bombardier beetle has glands that produce several chemicals which are released when the beetle is disturbed. The chemical mixture spews out hot and caustic, and the beetle can aim it with great accuracy to blind and burn ants or other predators that attack it.

Some of the compounds that beetles produce are amazingly potent. The blister beetle is a swollen, soft-bodied insect which lacks the hard, rigid wing covers and exoskeleton that protect other beetles. Instead, when molested, it leaks orange fluid from its leg joints, and as its name

tre-long tropical grasshoppers kick me with leg spines sharp enough to draw blood. But such insects are exceptions.

Insects that are conspicuous and cannot take escape actions have to be more aggressive in their defence. Social insects, like honeybees and hornets, for example, live in a large fixed nest. Because the nest is filled with young insects – a good source of protein – and sometimes honey, it is a rich, attractive food supply for predators. It is not surprising, then, that many social insects follow the strategy that "the best defence is a strong offence." Indeed, some social insects have been known to kill people.

Simply walking near a mound of fire ants will send them swarming out to bite and sting. I have been chased through a forest by killer bees, even though I had not come within five metres of their nest. These insects use stingers armed with powerful defensive chemicals to repel birds and mammals.

Milkweed bugs gather in dense groups, right, a behaviour that, in combination with their bold black-and-red colouring, makes them highly recognizable. Toxic to animals such as birds, these insects use number and appearance to signal their unpalatable taste to potential predators. These caterpillars, far right, have woven a silky retreat on a flower, which will help them avoid being detected by predators.

suggests, the fluid is so caustic, it can blister your skin. If swallowed, even the tiniest traces of the chemical can cause severe damage to kidneys.

Many other kinds of beetles produce toxic secretions. Often, these insects are relatively small and harmless-looking. Friends of mine have suffered severe skin burns from the secretions of tropical rove beetles no longer than a fingernail.

Insects may manufacture their own defensive compounds inside their bodies, but many insects collect chemicals from the plants upon which they feed. Monarch butterfly caterpillars, for example, eat milkweed plants and store their poisons in special glands. The poisons are retained when the caterpillar pupates and becomes a butterfly. If a bird eats a monarch butterfly, it vomits violently and thereafter avoids any butterfly that has the markings of a monarch.

The black-and-red milkweed bugs that feed on milkweed seeds also collect these defensive chemicals. When these bugs have fed on milkweed seeds, praying mantises will typically avoid them; but if the bugs are raised on sunflower seeds, which lack poisons, the mantises will eat them readily.

Monarch butterfly caterpillars are beautifully banded with black, yellow and white, and the adults are a conspicuous orange colour. This is no accident. Most of the insects that feed on milkweeds, including aphids, the tiger moth caterpillar and several kinds of beetles, have noticeable colour patterns.

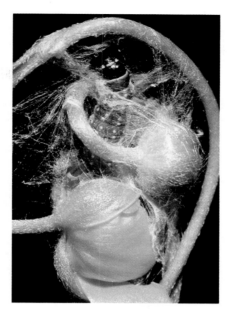

Many of these chemically defended insects live in groups, which makes them even more obvious. I have often seen clusters of brilliant blue, red and yellow stinkbugs that emit sprays of cyanide-based poisons. On poisonous nightshade plants, I have found masses of swollen, fat, leaf-eating beetle larvae that are black with reddish polka dots. If you grow potatoes, you will find their relatives in your garden—potato beetle larvae, which are bright pinkish orange with black dots. When you disturb these beetles, they excrete a foul orange toxic fluid from their mouths. The distinctive appearance of these poisonous insects is known as "warning coloration." It signals birds and other animals that the insects are poisonous.

Particular postures and conspicu-

ous behaviours also help communicate this message. I have watched caterpillarlike sawfly wasp larvae feeding on poplar leaves. Arranging themselves like curled candy canes all around the leaf edge, they flick back and forth when disturbed.

Delivering a warning can also be done with smell. In late summer, apple trees are often attacked by red-humped apple worms—strange, large, bristly humpbacked caterpillars. Their most obvious feature, however, is their smell. When you pick one up, it gives off a stench like concentrated vinegar that is noticeable probably even to birds, which lack a good sense of smell. If you poke a swallowtail caterpillar feeding on dill, parsley or anise, it extrudes a bright yellow Y-shaped organ from just behind its head region that emits a foul smell. The compound it uses is butyric acid, which has exactly the same scent as rancid butter or mammal sweat. Stinkbugs signal with a strong odour of bitter almonds that indicates the presence of cyanide. You can detect them just by brushing against the vegetation where they are sitting.

Your nose and eyes will do a good job of telling you which insects are equipped with these poisons. Well-defended insects usually have bright colours, a conspicuous appearance or an odour that is pungent and frequently unpleasant, even at a distance. Most of them are relatively harmless to humans, since we do not often eat them. But proceed with caution when handling an insect you know little about.

Life Cycles

The monarch butterfly, above, has just emerged from the pupal stage, right, during which the caterpillar's body was reorganized into the adult form. The monarch's pupal stage renders the insect immobile and vulnerable to predators and parasites, one disadvantage of the complete metamorphic life cycle. Insects with incomplete metamorphic life cycles keep growing and moving as they develop.

The mysterious transformation of a wormlike caterpillar to a pupa and then to a butterfly is one of nature's most amazing and beautiful feats.

The process of complete metamorphosis occurs not just in butterflies but in other groups of insects as well. Beetles, moths, flies, bees and wasps all develop through a series of life stages, each of which looks and acts differently. After hatching from eggs, these insects live as soft-bodied grubs, or larvae. When the larva has finished feeding and growing, it enters a resting state as a pupa, often in a protective outer encasement, or cocoon. During this phase, the adult structures develop. The adult emerges in a completely different form. Who could imagine that the fat white grub squirming in the soil would become a shiny June beetle?

One disadvantage of the complete metamorphic life cycle is the relative cost of the reorganization of the larval body into the adult form. For a caterpillar to become a butterfly, it must pass through a resting pupal stage, during which the tissues and organs are reorganized and the wings and limbs develop. Not only does this take energy, but in addition, the pupa cannot feed or move. Because this immobility makes them vulnerable to parasites and predators, insects with a pupal stage must devote time to finding a secure pupation site.

The advantage of complete metamorphosis is that it enables insects to live in radically different environments in their immature and adult stages. As a result, they also have distinct diets during these stages. Larvae grow and feed in the richest environment possible; the caterpillar of a butterfly, for example, is able to eat and digest leaves. The important necessities for adults often include the search for mates or breeding sites, a task that requires well-developed legs and wings. Wings also allow the butterfly to move from flower to flower so that it can feed on nectar and pollen.

Incomplete, or gradual, metamorphosis is common in insects such as bugs and grasshoppers. The immature individuals resemble adults, except they are smaller, have poorly developed wings and display different colours. But the key is that they usually live in the same environment and eat the same food as adults.

From species to species, insects differ greatly in the length of time they require to complete their life cycles. Generally, the smaller insects develop faster. A fruit fly may take only a few weeks to grow from an egg to an adult, while a large beetle may develop over a period of many years. Insects also vary in the time they spend in these stages. Tropical butterflies may live as adults for the better part of a year, probably somewhat longer than the time they spend as caterpillars. On the other hand, some Arctic moths live 14 years as caterpillars, although the caterpillars are active for just a few weeks each summer. The adult lives for one brief season, mates and then dies. Mayflies spend several years in streams as immature nymphs, then emerge as adults ready to mate, lay eggs and die, all on the same day.

Normally, insects appear at well-defined seasons. If you look at what kinds of moths gather around a porch light at night in spring, summer and fall, you will see a predictable sequence of species. Some are active early in spring and then vanish. Others are seen only in summer, and still others dominate during autumn. These differences are usually related to food availability and other ecological forces, such as the risk of being eaten by predators.

The life cycles of insects are sometimes highly synchronized over many years. Cicadas spend most of their lives underground eating plant roots. Few adults can be found flying around or feeding. But every 13 to 17 years, there is a massive hatch of adults. I have been near an oak tree in Georgia during just such an event. The tree was covered with cicadas sucking sap and buzzing their wings in a high-pitched whine that was so loud, I found it impossible to stand under the tree. These huge hatchings make it difficult for predators to eat more than a tiny proportion of the adults.

Insect life cycles influence and are influenced by the lives of other organisms and are therefore an important part of the year's changing seasons: the fresh leaves of spring stimulate insect growth that in turn determines the breeding cycle of forest songbirds. Learning about insect life cycles helps us to appreciate the relationships between living organisms and nature, which change and evolve each day as our planet spins its way around the sun in its annual cycle.

Diet

Many tiny caterpillars actually feed within leaves, above. After hatching from an egg inside the leaf, the caterpillar leaves a trail, or "leaf mine," that becomes wider as the caterpillar feeds and grows. Finally, it pupates and emerges as a flying moth. Because of a digestive specialization, the caterpillar of the tobacco hornworm moth, right, is able to feed on tomato leaves without being poisoned by the toxins in the foliage.

Insects eat almost anything that lives or was once alive, including people. I obtained firsthand experience of this when I discovered an insect living inside my arm. A botfly parasite had managed to attach its egg to a mosquito, and when the mosquito bit me, the botfly egg dropped onto my skin. Without my knowing it, the egg hatched and a tiny botfly maggot burrowed into the upper layers of skin on my arm. It was completely painless. I noticed only a bump, like a mosquito bite. After a few days, though, a distinct hole in the centre of the bump was visible. Shining a light into the hole, I spotted the tail end of the maggot. At first, I was intrigued, but my curiosity did not last. When the burrowing of the maggot grew painful, I gave up the experiment and poured rubbing alcohol over the opening, then carefully lifted the maggot out with fine tweezers.

The botfly had no choice about laying its egg on me. Like most insects, this type of botfly has a highly restricted diet. The only food it eats is either monkey or human.

The specializations of insect diet can be truly impressive. Some caterpillars and beetles live on a diet of carpets and woollen fabrics. In the desert, I have found beetles existing on nothing more than dry coyote fur. Tiny fairy wasps crawl underwater and swim through ponds and streams to attack damselfly eggs, because their larvae can develop only in these eggs. Fig wasps live inside fig fruits and feed solely on fig seeds. Fruit flies thrive on yeast. One group of moths drinks blood from around the eyes of oxen. One beetle feeds exclusively on the skin of beavers. Spongillaflies eat only freshwater sponges.

But not all insects have such specialized diets. Many are vegetarians, which is not surprising, given that the largest bulk of living biomass on Earth is plant life. Plants exist in many forms and in a great variety of shapes, both as green leafy material that is easy to digest and as woody material that is low in nutrients. Each of these plant resources supports a different set of insects. Some beetle larvae, moth caterpillars and fly maggots mine their way through the thin cross sections of leaves, creating distinctive swirling patterns. Other caterpillars and beetle larvae bore into the stems. Many beetle grubs feed only on the tissue under tree bark or in seedpods. Each plant usually offers a wide variety of diets to many kinds of insects.

Leaf-eaters, or folivores, include the larvae of many families of katydids and grasshoppers, beetles, butterflies and moths. Their chewing mouthparts are well suited to cutting and grinding foliage. The primary factor influencing the foliage-eating insects is plant chemistry: each plant contains hundreds of compounds, many of which are defensive poisons.

Insects respond to a plant's unique chemical composition by developing feeding specializations. For example, nicotine is a toxin found in tobacco plants. Only insects that can neutralize the poison, such as sphinx moth caterpillars, are able to eat tobacco leaves. If you find a caterpillar on a willow tree and want to raise it to an adult moth or butterfly, you will have to continue feeding it willow leaves. Oaks, maples and other tree species have such different chemistry that the caterpillar either will not feed or will be unable to grow normally. Only a few insects, such as gypsy moth caterpillars, can consume a wide range of plant leaves.

Wood often has fewer toxins than does foliage, but it is a lower-quality food and is difficult to digest. It is, nevertheless, an abundant food source, and the insects that feed on wood are among the most numerous of all animals. Termites dominate many parts of the Tropics, where they play a major role in breaking down woody debris.

The large beetles that bore through wood are among the most spectacular insects. In their larval form, the huge, brightly painted harlequin longhorn beetles and the giant Hercules and rhinoceros beetles grow longer than your hand and have powerful mouths. I have stood in a pine grove where the sound of beetles chewing was so loud, it was as though someone were eating a crisp celery stalk next to my ear. The wood-boring beetles often surprise homeowners by emerging from furniture or the timber in buildings years after the furniture or house was built. The larvae can take up to 10 years to work their way through the wood before metamorphosing into adults and crawling into the outside world.

Incidentally, because these beetles are so large and eat a relatively non-toxic diet, people often use them as food, especially in tropical forests. I myself have eaten beetle larvae and found them to be rather tasty when baked.

Sap sucking is another major insect feeding strategy that is well developed among insects such as aphids, cicadas, treehoppers, spittlebugs, leafhoppers and other assorted bugs that have tube-shaped mouthparts. Inserting their mouthparts into the plant's circulatory system, these insects extract nutrient-rich fluids. Sap-sucking insects can be serious pests. In addition to depriving the plant of the nutrients it may need to survive, many of these insects spread viruses from plant to plant.

Some bugs have turned their sucking mouthparts to a more nutritious food source – the blood of animals. Bedbugs, for example, feed on the blood of sleeping humans. The blood-sucking insects people know best are flies, including mosquitoes, sand flies, blackflies, deer flies and tsetse flies. To develop a large clutch of eggs, the females of these fly families often require a blood meal.

Scavenging is also an insect specialty. Because of their ability to fly and develop rapidly, some flies and beetles specialize in locating larger dead animals and laying their eggs and larvae on the rotting carcasses.

But perhaps the most common diet of insects is insects. Large numbers of insects are specialized predators and parasites of other insects, as we will see in the following two chapters.

The evolutionary success of many insects, such as yellow milkweed aphids, above right, is the result of their ability to feed on specialized groups of plants. The sap-sucking aphids, like this feeding stinkbug, far right, store plant poisons in their bodies that make them distasteful to predators.

Predators

Robber flies, above, are voracious predators of flying insects. These large-eyed flies perch and wait for prey to fly by, then pursue them and pounce on them from above. Grasping them with their basketlike array of legs, the robber flies impale and paralyze prey with their mouthparts. The praying mantis, right, ambushes insects by seizing them with its powerful spiny forelimbs.

Up close, a praying mantis looks as formidable as any *Tyrannosaurus rex*, a fierce predator in miniature. Its forelegs are long and armed with hooks and spines. Its giant eyes cunningly track every movement of passing insects, and its limbs lash out as fast as your eye can follow and pull the victim into its powerful jaws.

The praying mantis is a special kind of predator whose feeding strategy is something scientists call "sit-and-wait." Concealing itself in vegetation, it waits for a likely victim to pass by and then ambushes it. Such camouflaged predators are common in the animal world. Ambush bugs wait for bees and flies on flowers and impale them with their beaks, then inject them with a paralyzing saliva. A few look remarkably like harmless ants

and so trick the visiting bees into landing within range.

Some insect predators build traps to harvest prey. The ant lion larva creates a sand trap – a conical pit in loose, dry soil – and buries itself beneath the sand at the bottom of the pit. The slope of the pit is very steep, and when an ant or other insect enters, it inevitably slides to the bottom. When the insect tries to scramble up the unstable, crumbling slope, the ant lion flicks sand up to knock it down. Once the victim is within its grasp, the ant lion bites it with large, sharp mandibles. If you look carefully around an ant lion's pit, you will find the dried-up husks of its previous dinners.

Many predatory insects take a more active approach and go off in search of prey. Tiger beetles and carabid beetles run along the ground attacking insects as they go. I have seen the 2.5-centimetre-long black carabid caterpillar hunters moving through the forest killing tent caterpillars with fierce, energetic attacks. If you sit on a beach, you can often watch tiger beetles hunting along the sand. Catching one is a real challenge, but if you do, take a look at its huge eyes and large biting mouthparts – this is the equipment needed for effective hunting.

Highly mobile predators such as dragonflies are attracted to areas with lots of prey activity. Dragonflies that eat flies sometimes snatch the pesky deer flies and mosquitoes that harass large mammals. Some dragonfly species gather over ponds where clouds of midges are emerging. Passing back and forth like swallows, the dragon-flies pick their dinner out of the air. A few of the bigger dragonfly species attend such feeding frenzies to prey upon other dragonflies.

Some insects track their prey. Certain marsh fly larvae follow the slime trails of slugs, then attack them with a paralyzing toxin before eating them. Other predators use deception to lure their victims closer. One caterpillar in Hawaii tricks fruit flies into landing on its back. The upper side of the caterpillar is pigmented to resemble a fly. When a fruit fly lands, the cater-pillar rears backward, grabs its victim and devours it.

In the rainforests of Costa Rica, I have studied a large tropical rove bee-tle that has two methods of catching adult flies. The rove beetle often lands on a dead animal or a dung pile and waits for a fly to show up. When it does, the beetle lunges at the fly and impales it with its long mandibles. But when such fly-attracting resources are not available, the beetle impro-vises by manufacturing its own sweet and pungent-smelling chemical lure. Perched on a leaf, the beetle smears the surface with a pinkish white se-cretion from large glands located in its abdomen. It then turns to face the smear and lifts its tail, exposing the glands. Eventually, small flies are attracted. They land on the leaf and walk toward the beetle. When one is within a few millimetres, the beetle strikes, almost as a snake does, and quickly consumes the fly. Like most insect predation, it's not pretty, but it's undeniably interesting and dramatic.

Parasitism

Parasitoid wasps, such as the ichneumon seen in silhouette, above, patrol the vegetation looking for other insects to parasitize, which they do by laying their eggs inside them. The hundreds of white cocoons on the body of the sphinx moth caterpillar, right, contain braconid wasp pupae that fed as larvae inside the living caterpillar. When the wasps emerge, the caterpillar will die.

Caterpillars are hard to identify because many of them look alike. One surefire method is to raise them yourself, taking them from their habitat and keeping them in a cage of netting inside your house. By feeding them leaves from the same plant on which you found them, you can watch them create cocoons and eventually emerge as adults. Then it is much easier to figure out their species by their markings and coloration.

You don't always end up rearing a butterfly or a moth, however. Sometimes, when taking leaves to feed my caterpillars, I have found the cage buzzing with bristly flies or crawling with tiny wasps, the caterpillars lying dead. They have been killed by the flies or wasps, which were parasites living unseen inside their bodies.

Most insects play host to other insect parasites that live by eating their hosts. A large number of wasps and flies are parasitoids – insect parasites that kill their hosts slowly, rather than suddenly. Typically, a parasitoid wasp or fly lays its eggs or larvae on or within another insect. The parasite possesses the ability to feed selectively on the host insect's insides and to absorb its nutrients. In this way, the larvae gradually consume the body of their host, which usually dies just as the parasites mature.

The number of parasites a host caterpillar can support is staggering. You will often find caterpillars covered with the silk cocoons of the braconid wasps that have hatched out of the caterpillar. Their entire upper surface is coated with dozens, even hundreds, of cocoons all made by larvae that once lived inside the caterpillar.

If you could x-ray insects, you would discover that while many appear to be normal on the outside, they have parasitic insect larvae inside their bodies. As you attempt to rear butterfly or moth caterpillars, you will often find, as I did, that you are raising wasps or flies instead. Either the caterpillars you collected from the vegetation were already carrying parasites or the leaves you fed them had parasite eggs and larvae on them.

An insect can be attacked by a series of parasitoids that are, in turn, parasitized by other insects. As an example, consider the huge cigar-sized caterpillars of the cecropia moths. Not only do these caterpillars become infested with ichneumon wasp larvae

The female *Megarhyssa* ichneumon wasp, above right, can drill her ovipositor through several centimetres of solid wood to lay her eggs in the horntail wasp larvae that are feeding inside the tree. Female botflies deposit their eggs where they will come into contact with mammals. This species, far right, glues its eggs onto the root hairs that protrude from the burrows of chipmunks and other small mammals. When a chipmunk brushes against the roots, the eggs hatch, and the maggots burrow into the animal's body. Although botflies do not often kill their hosts, they leave them weakened.

(you can see black dots on the green caterpillar skin where the female wasps have injected their eggs), but they are parasitized by bristly tachina flies. The ichneumon wasps are then attacked by two other kinds of wasps, which are attacked by yet another wasp. A completely different set of these so-called hyperparasites also begins an assault on the tachinid larvae inside the caterpillar. The cecropia caterpillar you see feeding in a cherry tree might have six different species of wasp and fly larvae inside it.

Many parasitoids have had to evolve extraordinary delivery systems in order to insert their eggs into a living insect. The conopid flies that parasitize bumblebee workers can drill an egg into the hard-bodied bee with a sudden injection while the bee is in flight. Some tachina flies search out their caterpillar hosts and lay larvae directly on their bodies. Others merely broadcast eggs on leaves, which the caterpillars will swallow as they feed. Perhaps the most remarkable tachinids I have seen are those which fly ahead of army ant raids. Moving across the jungle floor, the swarming ants scare up large grasshoppers and katydids. As these insects leap into the air in flight, the tachina flies swoop down and parasitize them. In this way, tachinids take advantage of the behaviour of army ants as a convenient method of locating their victims.

In some wasps, the egg-laying organ, or ovipositor, has been adapted to bore through wood. I have watched *Megarhyssa* ichneumon wasps drill through several centimetres of solid elm in order to parasitize the wood-boring larvae of horntail wasps that feed deep inside dead trees. The parasite appears to detect the presence of horntails by smelling with its antennae and perhaps by feeling the larvae's vibrations in the wood. The ovipositor of *Megarhyssa* is longer than the wasp itself – it measures almost 10 centimetres – and is highly flexible. The wasp not only is able to insert the ovipositor through several centimetres of wood but also uses it to inject eggs into its horntail host.

Many parasitoid insects are important biological-control agents used to prevent crop damage by insect pests. Large numbers of wasps that act as insect-egg parasites are released in orchards and fields every year. Each female wasp can parasitize hundreds of pest-insect eggs and thus provide effective nontoxic pest control.

A large number of insects feed as parasites on animals such as mammals and birds. Lice, fleas and even some beetles and flies specialize in the skin and blood of birds and mammals. Birds have lice that live inside their feathers, and their nests are often infested with lice. In fact, one rea-

son birds do not always reuse nests year after year may be the buildup of lice and fleas that would result. The presence of these parasites might also explain why birds take dust baths and sometimes smear themselves with the defensive chemicals excreted by ants, which they nab with their bills. Such actions may help kill or repel fleas and lice.

The insects that feed as external parasites are known as ectoparasites, and they usually live on the outside of their hosts. Occasionally, they take up residence under the skin. While working in tropical rainforest, I have had toe fleas living inside my feet and botflies in my arm until I was able to remove them with tweezers. Botflies do not have much of an effect on humans, but when they infest small

mammals like chipmunks and deer mice, these large flies can have a disastrous impact.

Bloodsucking insects also include highly mobile ectoparasites, such as blackflies, mosquitoes, sand flies, deer flies and stiletto flies, as well as moderately mobile parasites like bedbugs. Once these parasites have taken a blood meal, they leave their host. Normally, only females that must manufacture a huge supply of eggs feed heavily on mammalian blood. Bloodsucking flies can render large areas of land uninhabitable for people, either because they transmit fatal diseases such as sleeping sickness or because they are just so abundant and voracious that they make outdoor living a nightmare. Anyone who has hiked near a Canadian lake during blackfly season knows exactly what I am talking about.

Certain types of bloodsucking insects sometimes feed on other insects. I have watched large butterfly caterpillars being bitten by tiny sand flies, and some of the sand flies will likewise tap into the wing veins of dragonflies to feed.

Insects that manage to escape parasitism by other insects do have enemies, however. A large number of small organisms, such as bloodsucking mites, are known to attack insects. These internal parasites include nematode worms and many microscopic protozoans. Perhaps the knowledge that all insects suffer parasitism will be some consolation when you are struggling unsuccessfully to dodge a crowd of bloodthirsty mosquitoes.

27

Locomotion

Insects such as this honeybee, above, are the most accomplished flying animals ever to evolve. Because of their light weight and sophisticated wing design, they can hover and manoeuvre with great agility and efficiency. Whirligig beetles, right, have legs modified for both diving into and sculling across the water. They are unable to walk effectively on land, but if removed from the water, they will launch into flight and find a new water source.

One of my most vivid memories of the highlands of Guatemala, Central America, is of a ride I once took in a minibus that was crammed to the roof with people. When I had finally disentangled myself from the mass of humans and squeezed into a seat, I noticed that the air was filled with black specks. It was almost as though someone were tossing handfuls of black pepper about. What I was actually looking at were fleas, hundreds of fleas, rocketing wildly from one traveller to the next. As the minibus wound its way through the mountains, I entertained myself by observing just how far the small flattened insects could leap.

Nothing on Earth can leap farther for its size: a flea is able to make jumps that are more than 100 times its body length. And it can do so over and over again. One researcher demonstrated that rabbit fleas could leap once every second for three straight days without stopping.

The flea owes its incredible leaping abilities to two things: the first is a specialized set of leg muscles; the second is a rubbery pad of protein called resilin that is located in the flea's hind legs. The leg muscles apply pressure to the pad. When the pressure is suddenly released, the pad powerfully extends the hind legs and propels the flea great distances.

As those of us who have dogs or cats know, a flea does more than hop – it also crawls expertly through animal fur, a mode of locomotion made easy by its flattened body shape. Like fleas, most insects use several differ-ent techniques for moving about their environment.

Terrestrial insects such as beetles and bugs are usually able to walk or hop as well as fly. Although it is a time-consuming method of locomotion, walking is a relatively energy-efficient way of getting around. Flight, while speedy – most insects can fly at about four metres per second – is, by comparison, energy-expensive. A flying insect burns 50 times as much energy as the amount it uses when it is at rest. Nevertheless, some insects are specialized for flight. Dragonflies and sphinx moths, for example, move almost entirely by flying, and they do so with great agility. Displaying all the manoeuvres of a helicopter, they can hover up and down and even move backward.

Despite the drawback of its excessive use of energy, flight does offer flying insects an important advantage: it enables the insect to generate huge amounts of body heat. Large sphinx moths, bumblebees and some scarab beetles are actually able to raise their body temperature simply by exercising their flight muscles. In cold weather, they can produce enough heat to allow them to be active while smaller insects or insects that walk are unable to move about. If you happen to disturb a resting bumblebee worker in the flower garden one cool morning, take a close look. You will notice the worker's abdomen pulsing in and out with the effort of contracting its muscles as it warms up for flight.

Because flight is not always an ad-

28

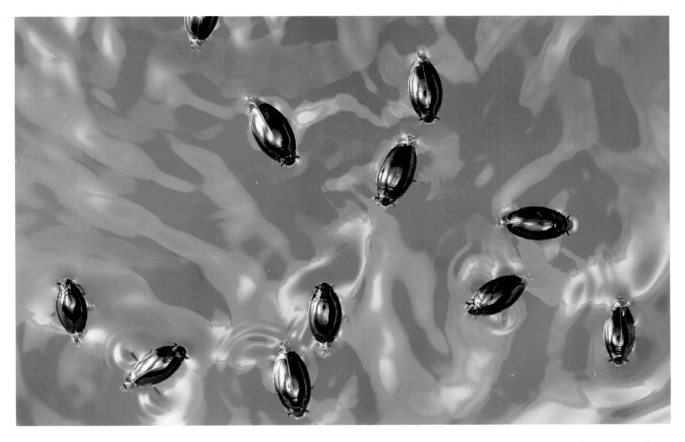

vantage, many insects have adapted to their habitats over time by no longer developing wings. Sometimes, only flightless forms of insects can be found in caves or on cold, windy mountaintops – habitats that make flying difficult. Yet wings are a necessity for species such as water striders that live on small temporary ponds and streams. Once the ponds dry up, these insects must be able to fly to a new habitat. The water striders that live on oceans, which never dry up, do not have this problem, and as a result, all the marine water striders have lost their wings.

A few insects have even lost the ability to walk or squirm their way along. Instead, they rely on passive forms of dispersal. Legless scale insects are carried from plant to plant by the wind or by ants. Other insects hitch rides on the bodies of larger insects. I have found tiny parasitic wasps travelling about clamped onto the hairy abdomens of butterflies.

Many insects, such as water beetles, swim superbly, using legs that have been modified to act as oars. The dragonfly larva swims by squirting jets of water from its abdomen. Perhaps the most unusual way of getting around is demonstrated by the semi-aquatic rove beetle. Jumping onto the surface of the pond, this beetle excretes a chemical which reacts so violently with water that the insect is sent skimming across the pond at high speed.

Migration and Navigation

In autumn, millions of monarch butterflies fly south from North America to overwinter in coniferous forests in the mountains of Mexico. Destruction of this winter habitat by illegal logging, however, has endangered the monarch population.

During the late-summer and early-autumn months, many insect populations retreat into the ground. Crawling deep inside crevices and hiding under bark, they are looking for safe places to pass the winter. Most of these insects carry strong antifreeze compounds in their blood that prevent the formation of damaging ice crystals, even at temperatures far below zero. Insects that lack these abilities use another strategy – they migrate. Just like many songbirds, they fly to less stressful climates.

The migrations of the large orange-and-black-patterned monarch butterflies are the best known and the most colourful. There are two monarch migratory populations in North America. The western population heads to the sunny and mild climate of coastal California for the winter, while the eastern-central population flies thousands of kilometres south, into the mountains of central Mexico. In the mountains, the monarchs congregate by the millions in forests, where they hang in huge orange clusters on the branches of sheltered conifers.

Flight is a costly activity for insects, and the monarchs must build up a store of body fat to help them undertake the strenuous trek to warmer climes. The fat also enables them to survive a long winter when feeding is not always possible. As spring arrives in the north and the new milkweed plants emerge, the monarchs make the journey back.

Other milkweed-eating insects, such as the large milkweed bug, also make a north-south migration. Shorter days, cooler temperatures and declining food sources stimulate the bugs to launch into migratory flights to the southern United States.

The end of the growing season is not the sole reason for moving. Rather than migrating because food plants are not available in winter, ladybugs move because the aphids they eat disappear. People engaged in aphid control have collected ladybugs in buckets to distribute to gardeners only to find that once the aphid population has been diminished, the ladybugs have a strong urge to fly to a more plentiful food supply.

There is also a phenomenon related to migration that involves the mass movements of insects such as locusts. When, as a result of favourable weather, these grasshoppers build up large populations, their hormones undergo a change, and the adults begin to throng together. Reproductive cycles become synchronized, and the locusts feed voraciously as they strip the landscape bare of vegetation.

Although in North America, the Rocky Mountain locust appears to have become extinct, migratory locusts are still common in Africa, where they regularly destroy millions of dollars' worth of cropland. Swarms up to 10 billion strong have been recorded flooding across the landscape, covering hundreds of square kilometres. Unlike monarchs, the locusts may never return to their birthplace, but the ecological principle guiding their migration is similar. Moving is sometimes worth the energy expended, especially when the food supply disappears.

Part of the life cycle of many insects is a dispersal phase, a period when they travel long distances. Dispersal allows new individuals to begin reproductive life well removed from the parental colony, a situation that prevents competition, reduces the prospect of transmitting disease to the next generation and lowers the probability of inbreeding by otherwise nonmigratory, or sedentary, insects. The dispersal phase also provides a means of locating new food sources.

Certain insects such as aphids spend much of the growing season wingless, but as the end of summer approaches, the adults develop wings and disperse. Gallflies grow wings in every second generation as part of a cycle of sexual reproduction and dispersal. In the case of scale insects, usually only males develop wings.

Insects such as water beetles and water striders that thrive in short-lived habitats like temporary ponds virtually always have an adult dispersal phase. The adults have well-developed flight muscles, but after they relocate, they often digest their own wing muscles and use the nutrients for other tasks, like reproduction.

All insects are able to orient themselves using light, wind and gravity – elements that guide the insect in the proper direction. Orientation behaviour is relatively easy to observe. If a flying insect gets into your house or you trap one in a bottle, its usual escape response is to fly toward the brightest area. By contrast, soil insects such as burrowing crickets or cockroaches scurry to the darkest areas.

More demanding movements – migration or going to and from a nest on foraging trips, for example – also require proper orientation. The insect must navigate a route, and for it to do so, it needs complex information.

For instance, how does a mud dauber – a wasp that builds a nest of mud, then fills it with caterpillars, other insects and spiders to feed hatching larvae – find its way from the hunting grounds back to the nest? It uses several sources of information. Memorizing landmarks such as the pattern of trees on the horizon and of the vegetation near the nest is one strategy. The wasp also uses the sun as a combination compass and watch. An amazing built-in mechanism en-ables wasps and bees to adjust their flight patterns according to the changing position of the sun in the sky. But what happens on cloudy days?

Many insects do not depend on a direct view of the sun because they can see polarized ultraviolet light. When light travels from the sun to Earth, it moves in straight lines. Insects can see not only these directional planes – sort of like seeing a sunbeam – but also ultraviolet light, which is invisible to us. Ultraviolet light is so powerful, it penetrates even thick clouds. Using ultraviolet light and its polarized orientation, bees and wasps are able to determine the sun's position in the sky.

There is also evidence indicating that honeybees, sensing the magnetic fields surrounding Earth, orient their flight according to the magnetic lines of force. In fact, bees have about 100 million tiny magnets – concentrations of the mineral magnetite, or lodestone – embedded in certain tissues, and these may act as magnetic sensors.

When you watch insects going about their activities, remember that they see and hear and smell things which humans cannot detect. How do wild honeybees living in a hollow tree know where their hive is as they fly over a forest of thousands of similar trees? How do monarch butterflies instinctively know in which direction Mexico lies? How do they sense the right time to fly south? What signals guide them? We have a lot to learn about how insects use their simple brains to find their way through a complex environment.

Courtship and Reproduction

The female grasshopper on the left, above, is larger than her mate, a pattern that is typical for insects which lay huge numbers of eggs. Courtship for praying mantises, right, is a potentially dangerous affair for males: the female, often bigger and more powerful than the male, has been known to treat the male as prey, devouring him after mating.

In early spring, when the sun is shining brightly but the trees are still bare, mourning cloak butterflies are already active. You can watch them on their wild chases through the forest. In this courtship ritual, the female leads and the male follows as they climb in the air, spiralling higher and higher, then suddenly dive downward. Only if the male is persistent and able to keep up with the female will she eventually settle on the ground and allow him to mate with her.

Courtship and reproduction are among the most important activities any individual undertakes, and insects, like many organisms, devote much time and energy to these events. Butterfly courtship is usually drawn out, with the male chasing the female and occasionally displaying special scales on his wings for her benefit. All summer long, you can hear the sounds of insect courtship; the whine of cicadas, the chirping of crickets and the ratcheting nighttime noise of katydids are all male courtship songs designed to attract females.

Sometimes, both a visual display and a song are combined. In late summer, I like to watch the courtship displays of Carolina locusts – large, mottled grey-brown grasshoppers that prefer open sandy areas for egg laying. The males leap into the air and hover a few metres above the ground, beating and showing off their hind wings, which are black with a broad yellow border. Then they produce a high-pitched rasping song. When they finally settle to the ground, the females hop or fly in and land beside them. At that point, the males flaunt their banded legs, kicking them conspicuously back and forth. Eventually, mating takes place between the pair, and the female lays her eggs in the soil.

There is a wide range of courtship and mating systems in the insect world, and they vary according to the ecology of the insect. Midges, mayflies, March flies, ants and other insects that emerge in huge numbers are involved in a massive scramble for mates. Compared with the elaborate rituals performed by butterflies, their courtship is fairly straightforward. Males join together in busy dancing clouds. These mating swarms are located near some landmark, sometimes over the top of a tree or in a patch of bright sunlight. The females simply fly into the swarm, and the first male to contact a female becomes her mate.

Males that mate in swarms often have a special mating structure which locks the male to the female so that rival males cannot separate them. The mating apparatus of the male honeybee actually explodes and detaches, plugging the newly mated queen and preventing other males from mating with her. A number of insects, including butterflies, have chemical mating plugs which serve the same purpose and may even provide nutrients that the female absorbs and uses for egg production.

Typically, males pursue females, and the behaviours they exhibit are designed to increase their chances of finding a partner. In the case of many

butterflies and flies, males simply congregate on hilltops, where females can conveniently find them. As experienced insect collectors know, the best way to find lots of insects in early summer is to climb the highest hill in the area.

In some species of butterflies and flies, the male perches on leaves along trails and streambanks and waits for a female to fly by. When that happens, the male aggressively pursues the female. If another male passes through, it is usually chased off. Males also search out females at known feeding sites, such as the flowering shrubs which attract the female flies, wasps, bees, butterflies and beetles that feed on nectar and pollen.

Fruit flies and many kinds of small beetles congregate at the pockets of fermenting sap that collect on wounded trees. You can also find them wherever there is rotting fruit or masses of mushrooms. In these situations, feeding, courtship and mating all take place at once. Put out an overripe banana or dab a fermented solution of brown sugar and yeast on a tree trunk, and you can organize one of these congregations yourself. The behaviour of fruit flies can be particularly entertaining. If you sit close to the bait and are careful not to disturb the flies by breathing on them or moving suddenly, you can see males flicking their wings in courtship displays and butting their heads against male rivals.

In some species, there is an even more direct relationship between feeding and courtship. Males court females by presenting them with food, in the form of "nuptial gifts." Male scorpion flies and dance flies catch other insects and present them to the females. As the female feeds on the insects, the male mates with her.

Females may also have behaviours that attract males. Some female moths release chemical scents that can draw males from great distances.

Many larger and longer-lived insects are truly territorial, defending a space or resources that have proved to be attractive to reproductive females. I have studied the territorial behaviour of the black-winged damselfly, which lives by small woodland streams. When the females are ready to reproduce, they search for sections of stream with floating weeds and other vegetation into which they drill their eggs as a means of protecting them. The male damselfly establishes a territory in these regions by monopolizing a portion of the stream and chasing off other males that approach. Some of these aerial battles can last for almost an hour. The victorious male then mates with any females that attempt to lay their eggs in the area.

An alternative to defending an entire territory is for a male simply to guard the female. Some male dragonflies and damselflies fly linked in tandem with the female to prevent other males from harassing and mating with her. Often, the male remains attached to the female for several days, until the eggs are fertilized. (This behaviour is also exhibited by many of the true bugs, such as stinkbugs.) Some of the bright blue damselfly species have a system in which the female descends underwater to lay eggs, dragging her mate with her.

A pond during summer is a great place to begin your observation of insect courtship and reproduction. Can you tell which insects are territorial? Do they always return to the same perch after each chase and battle? There is a simple but effective way to keep track of some insects' activities. For example, gently net a male dragonfly. (You can identify the male by the pair of claspers on the tip of its abdomen.) Then, very carefully, use a felt-tipped pen or thin enamel paint and a toothpick to mark him with a distinctive spot on the wing or thorax. That spot will permanently identify him. I have seen marked males show up at the same spot for two months, while others disappear the same day. After you spend time watching insects courting, you will begin to realize that each insect displays its own individual behaviours, and there's a lot of fun to be had in getting to know them.

Mating postures of insects such as this pair of damselflies, above right, can be complex. The bright blue male carries the female in tandem until they locate a site in which the female can lay her eggs. This ritual prevents other males from mating with the female. Flag-footed bugs, far right, may remain locked in copulation for many hours, a process that allows the male to fertilize the female's eggs without genetic competition from other males.

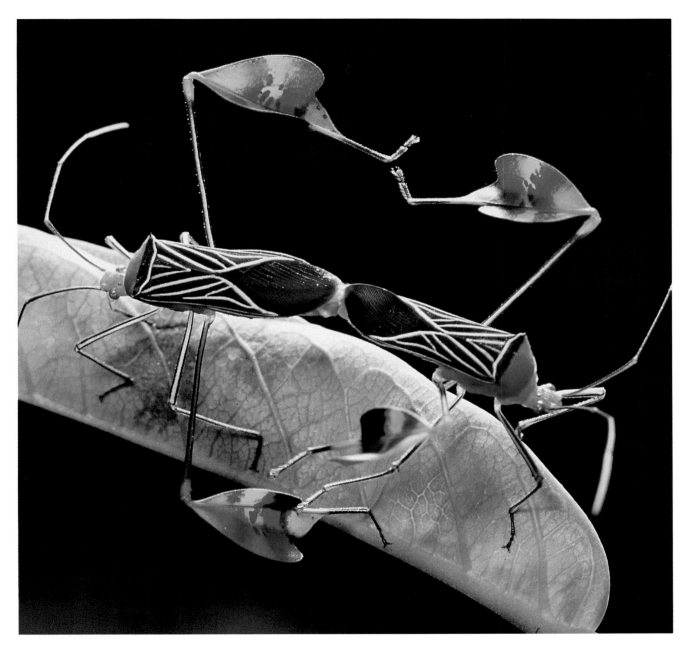

Parental Care

The male giant water bug allows his mate to attach her eggs to his wing covers, where they will be protected from predators and can be exposed to the air periodically.

On a warm summer day, you can watch dragonflies swooping low over a pond or a slow-moving stream. Some of them are hunting or chasing mates or rivals. But others are performing a curious ritual. Hovering and flying across the surface, they dip their abdomens into the water every few seconds. You may also see the more delicate, bright blue damselflies touch down and crawl underwater. They are laying eggs.

Dragonflies typically lay hundreds of eggs by dropping them into the water and leaving them to hatch by themselves. Although many will be eaten or washed away by the current, it is a successful reproductive strategy that is based on producing large numbers of eggs, then providing no care after they are deposited.

In the same pond or stream, you will be able to find insects that have a completely different reproductive strategy. Giant water bugs lurk among the waterweeds, waiting to catch tadpoles and small fish with their powerful forelegs. Brown and flattened, these bugs are the same size and shape as dried-up leaves. If you look at enough of them, you will eventually find one that has row upon row of barrel-shaped, light-coloured eggs glued onto its protective wing covers. This is a male carrying eggs that a female has deposited on his back. The strategy of these bugs is to produce just a few large eggs and to provide them with a great deal of parental care. The male giant water bug has a powerful puncturing bite that he uses to defend himself. To ensure that the eggs are safe from most predators, the male carries them with him. He also keeps the eggs near the surface of the pond so that they have a good supply of oxygen. The result of all this care is that large numbers of eggs will hatch.

Some insects have evolved a parental-care method that is based on carrying the developing larvae inside their bodies. This method is in sharp contrast to that used by insects such as houseflies, which simply broadcast thousands of tiny eggs wherever there is rotting garbage. In the tsetse fly, for example – the blood-feeding insect that transmits sleeping sickness in Africa – a single egg hatches into a maggot inside the female's body, where it grows larger and larger as the mother feeds on the blood of game animals or, sometimes, humans. Only when the maggot fills its mother's abdomen does she release it onto the soil. The larva then burrows down and pupates immediately.

Insects also vary greatly in the amounts of food they provide their offspring. Groups such as butterflies and moths, mayflies, caddis flies and stone flies tend to deposit their eggs and abandon them. Some insects, like earwigs, various mantids and sawflies, remain with their eggs and will attack any insects that venture near, but they do not feed their offspring. Other insects, including bees, ants and beetles, have a form of parental care that is based on providing nests with food. Many wasps, such as tarantula hawks, mud daubers and potter wasps, and bees such as leafcutters invest resources in their offspring before they hatch. These insects build a protected nest or a burrow and provision it with enough food for their larvae to feed on so that they can develop safely in the nest.

The tarantula hawk, for example, is a large-winged wasp that lives in deserts and tropical forests. Before the female is ready to reproduce, she digs a burrow deep into the soil. Then she begins to hunt, moving rapidly across the ground. When she encounters a tarantula, a battle ensues. The tarantula defends itself by using its long legs to fend off the wasp and attempting to bite her with its sharp fangs. Eventually, the wasp manoeuvres her flexible abdomen under the tarantula's body and paralyzes the

spider with her powerful sting. Dragging the stunned tarantula down into its burrow, the wasp deposits a single egg on the spider. The wasp then leaves, closing the burrow with soil. When the egg hatches, it has a huge and secure store of food. The larva feeds on the paralyzed spider until it is ready to pupate and emerge as an adult wasp.

The food-storage system is well developed in other insects too. Potter wasps push paralyzed caterpillars into small mud pots before laying their eggs inside, while leafcutter bees make leaf-lined cells in hollow twigs that they fill with nectar and pollen for their larvae. This strategy depends on finding a concentrated resource that can be collected and stored in a safe place. Since the leaves, roots and decaying debris which scarab beetles such as Japanese and June beetles feed on are not particularly nutritious, these insects do not bother with that kind of parental care. By contrast, scarab beetles that feed on highly nutritious carrion or dung provision their nests with those foods. Dung beetles often carve away a piece of dung and deposit it in a deep burrow, where it will serve as food for their larvae. The parent may remain within the burrow for months, tending the nest to keep fungus from growing on the food supply.

Burying beetles feed on dead mice and shrews. Usually, one beetle hunts out a mouse carcass – perhaps one that has been dropped by an owl – and then sends out a sense signal known as a pheromone which

leads its mate to the site. Together, the male and the female bury the mouse, chewing and reshaping it into a nest. They tend this underground nest and feed their larvae by regurgitating the chewed-up mouse.

The most extreme example of parental care I have ever seen is exhibited by the thornlike *Umbonia* treehopper. When a female is ready to reproduce, she selects a twig on a special kind of legume tree. Using her ovipositor, she cuts two parallel slits about one centimetre long in the bark, into which she inserts her eggs. Then she straddles the eggs, gripping the bark securely with her legs. If any ants, beetles or wasps approach, she charges at them, buzzing her wings violently. If they get close enough, she kicks the intruders with her powerful hind legs.

When the eggs are about to hatch into nymphs, the female cuts a series of holes in a neat spiral down the twig. These feeding holes allow the nymphs to insert their mouthparts into the twig and feed on tree sap. The female stays with the nymphs for up to two months, defending them vigorously and providing them with new feeding holes until they mature into adults. Virtually her entire life is dedicated to rearing just one set of offspring.

Many people are surprised to find that insects can be attentive, highly devoted parents. But parental behaviour is like most other aspects of insect behaviour: if you take the time to observe insects, you will continue to be impressed by their versatility.

Habitat and the Environment

Springtails, above, are one of the few groups of insects that have been able to colonize and use special microhabitats in winter. During the cold weather, springtail colonies flourish on moss, fungus and even snow. Rainforest katydids, such as this leaf-mimicking species, right, are restricted to a warm, wet environment and cannot survive outside that habitat.

It was late July, but the mountain ridge was still capped with snow and ice. I was hiking the Coast Mountains in northern British Columbia, and it was thirsty work in spite of the cool climate. I filled my water bottle with pure glacier water running right from the melting ice and raised it to drink. At that moment, I saw the water's surface alive with purple insects. Tiny springtails just a couple of millimetres long were flipping about, using special forklike spring levers under their abdomens. Also known as "snow fleas," springtails feed on the red algae that grow on the surface of the glacier. When I looked at the snow, I could see the red-stained depressions that were the feeding grounds for millions of springtails. Even in a land of ice and rock, insects abound.

The harshest deserts and the wettest tropical rainforests all provide habitat, or living space, for insects. Even far out to sea on the open ocean surface, water striders can be found skating on the waves.

Generally, the more extreme the habitat, the fewer insects it will support. Very dry or cold habitats have fewer insects than warm, moist habitats such as tropical rainforests. Springtails, for example, are the only insect species I have seen living on a glacier, but sitting quietly in a tropical rainforest or even in a hardwood forest in Canada, I can spot dozens, possibly hundreds, of insect species.

The variety of food and microclimates available in a habitat is what most affects insect diversity. A forest provides more habitats than a cornfield. A canyon has more habitats than a flat stretch of sandy desert. A weedy vacant lot offers more habitats than a neatly mowed lawn.

Most insects have special adaptations that make them suited to life in a particular habitat. Desert insects frequently have heavy, waterproof exoskeletons to protect them from wind, dry heat and the harsh ultraviolet rays of the sun. By contrast, cave insects are often soft, pale, blind and adapted to mild, humid, perpetually dark habitats.

If a habitat is very specialized, the insects that are adapted to it are usually unable to survive outside it. The crickets that live beside glaciers, for example, are adapted to permanently cool temperatures and can actually die from the warmth of a human hand picking them up. Few insects are *that* specialized, but many are restricted to distinct living spaces.

Most insects live in a specific part of their environment, referred to as a microhabitat. Certain weevils and other kinds of beetles spend their entire larval lives inside a single seed. Both the nature of the food and the microclimate factors, such as humidity levels, that insects encounter in the seedpod are important influences on their habitat choice.

Even a relatively small wildflower offers a great variety of insect microhabitats. Consider the pitcher plant, a carnivorous, or meat-eating, plant found in Canadian bogs. What counts as a habitat for the insects associated with these plants depends on the scale of observation. The general hab-

itat, or macrohabitat, for pitcher plant insects is the peat bog where the plants grow. But each of the various pitcher plant insect species lives in a specialized part of the plant.

The exposed leaves are eaten by a unique kind of cutworm. Another type of cutworm bores in perpetual darkness and damp, chewing through the roots. A moth caterpillar feeds on the hard, dry seeds. A flesh fly larva lives in the water trap, as does a mosquito and a midge, and they are all

adapted to withstand the digestive enzymes that the plant excretes to break down the terrestrial insects it captures in the water trap. Each insect occupies a different position in the water trap. Most important, none of the insects can live anywhere else but in these exact spots.

You can find different insect microhabitats wherever you look. A single tree in a forest has several microhabitats on its trunk alone. The north side of a tree, being shadier, cooler and

moister, supports more moss, lichens and the caterpillars that eat them than the south side, which is used by other insects. When you walk through the woods, look at the sunny sides of the trees. There, day-active butterflies, dragonflies and flies bask in the light. On the shady north side, you will see moths resting. Hidden by day, they are waiting for their nighttime activities to begin. Similar trees that grow on the windy exposed edge of the forest present microhabitats which

Within any habitat, there are many microhabitats that insects are able to exploit. *Acanthomyops* ants, right, nest under stones that are exposed to the sun. They pile their grublike white larvae under the stone, and the warmth of the sun-heated rock speeds up the development of the larvae. South American leaf-cutting ants, far right, nest deep in the soil, and the stable, moist microhabitat of the nest enables them to culture mushrooms for food.

are different from those found on the same species of tree in the forest interior.

It is not only plants that offer living microhabitats. Animals provide food and shelter for many insects as well. Each kind of mammal and bird supports its own insect community. Fur, feathers and skin are microhabitats for lice, fleas and other parasitic insects, all of which tend to specialize in certain host species.

Soil is also a habitat rich in insects. Each type of soil and each layer of soil supports different insects. Sandy soils may have ant lion nests and many kinds of ants. Peat and other highly organic soils, while lacking ant lions, instead have springtails or the wiry larvae of click beetles that feed on plant matter. Life on the surface of the soil differs from that found in its depths. The upper surface layers are patrolled by mobile insects, such as predatory carabid and rove beetles, that actively hunt for other insects, while the deeper subsoil is penetrated only by insects such as cicadas and their larvae, that burrow deeply in search of tree roots, whose fluids they suck. A simple stone laid on the ground can provide a microhabitat. Ants will use it as an incubator, placing their larvae and pupae in chambers underneath it. The heat from the sun-warmed stone speeds the development of the immature ants.

The specialization that most insects have for a particular habitat and its features makes them extremely vulnerable to habitat disturbance. Human activities are steadily decreasing the number of different habitats by converting them into cities and farms. Agricultural pests and a few cockroaches flourish in human habitats, but such human-associated insects are just a tiny fraction of the number of species found in natural habitats. Even though the land may still be there when a forest is cut or a prairie is ploughed or a bog is drained, the original habitat and its special inhabitants are gone.

What happens when we lose insects and their habitats? Insects are one of the most important components of almost every terrestrial eco-

system. Without insects, most flowers would go unpollinated. As a result, we would not have honey, fruits like apples and apricots or nuts such as almonds, all of which require healthy bee populations for pollination.

Efforts intended to create habitats are often unsuccessful. When farmers tried to grow Brazil nuts commercially, they cut down tropical rainforest and planted Brazil nut trees in rows, plantation-style. But these trees depend on orchid bees for pollination, and without the natural orchids of the rainforest, there were not enough orchid bees in the plantations. Hence no nuts were produced.

Insects also play an important role in circulating nutrients through the ecosystem. Flies and beetles rapidly dispose of dung, carrion and rotting vegetation. When Australians introduced sheep, cattle and other large grazing mammals to their country, they immediately encountered a problem: there were no native dung beetles to bury cow and sheep dung in the soil. Millions of hectares of pasture became unusable until dung beetles were brought from Africa.

The list of ecological services that insects provide is a long one. Termites and beetles, for example, convert woody debris into concentrated insect protein that feeds birds and other predators. The residue these insects leave behind creates more fertile soil. Ants also dig through and aerate the soil. Without such insects, our forests would be much less productive and far less beautiful.

Insects are no more and no less necessary than the other species – the birds, mammals, plants and all the other organisms that make up an ecosystem. Does it matter whether we lose bogs and those specialized pitcher plants? That loss alone would not cause an ecological disaster, but it would make the world a poorer and less interesting place in which to live. More important is the total and growing effect of losing habitats and species. Species that become extinct can never be replaced, and it is almost impossible to re-create natural habitats once they have been destroyed.

If we want healthy ecosystems which will continue to produce all the useful and interesting elements of nature, we must preserve the habitats that all organisms, including insects, depend on for survival.

Aquatic Insects

Aquatic insects, such as this giant water bug nymph feeding on a minnow, above, are often the dominant predators in small ponds, while backswimmer bugs, right, live upside down, drawing air from the surface of the pond and using their oarlike legs to scull through the water.

In ice-cold rushing mountain streams, in tiny puddles that collect in tree holes and crotches, at the bottom of deep lakes, on the wet mossy rock faces of waterfalls—wherever there is fresh water—insects can be found. In fact, about 5 percent of all insects spend much of their time in water, and many of the major groups of insects—mayflies, stone flies, caddis flies, dragonflies—are almost exclusively aquatic as larvae. A large number of beetles, dobsonflies and other bugs and flies are also aquatic.

Aquatic insects enjoy the advantage of living in environments such as marshes that often teem with other life forms. As an added benefit, many aquatic habitats—temporary ponds, for example—are relatively free of insect predators like fish. Insects evolved on land, however, and therefore have a respiratory system that was intended for breathing air. Likewise, their bodies were originally designed for walking and flying. To be successful in water, aquatic insects have had to adapt physically to this dense, oxygen-poor medium.

It is easy to see such adaptations. If you catch diving water beetles or water bugs, you will find that they are highly streamlined. Many of the big diving beetles are as sleek as a sailboat's hull. Their legs are often modified so that the hairs and limb segments resemble oars or paddles.

Because of the nature of their respiratory systems, aquatic insects have had to evolve a variety of means of either gaining access to the air or extracting oxygen directly from the wa-

ter. Many simply come to the surface every few minutes and expose a breathing tube to the atmosphere. The rat-tailed maggot got its name from the long, thin breathing tube that it extends to the water's surface like a snorkel.

Some beetles and bugs have an air bubble stuck to their bodies. When they dive, the air bubble acts as a kind of gill that absorbs oxygen from the water and releases carbon dioxide. Insects like blackflies, mayflies and stone flies that live in fast-flowing streams have a filament—a flat, flaplike structure—which acts in the same manner, exchanging respiratory gases with the water. Midge larvae living in muddy lake bottoms have evolved haemoglobin, the same oxygen-carrying red pigment that makes our blood red. The pigment not only gives the midge larvae a bright pink appearance but helps them obtain adequate oxygen.

The majority of aquatic insects develop underwater as immature larvae or nymphs, then live their adult stages in the terrestrial environment. This makes sense for several reasons. Moving and breathing underwater is relatively easy for a long, skinny larva or nymph. But finding a mate and a new habitat often requires flight. When the aquatic insects are ready, they simultaneously leave the water in what is called a mass emergence. While this leave-taking signifies a new chapter in the life history of such insects as blackflies, mayflies and stone flies, it also presents an irresistible feeding opportunity to their pred-

Many aquatic insects, such as these mayflies, above right, emerge in immense swarms of adults, ready to mate. As the swarms move toward the surface of the water, they provide food for trout and other fish. Once they are in flight, the insects become food for foraging birds, bats and dragonflies. The mosquitoes that live inside a rainwater-filled plant in the rainforest, far right, are able to breed in small temporary bodies of water which lack predatory fish. Like most aquatic insects living in still water, the mosquitoes must have access to air for respiration.

ators. Fish nab the insects as they rise to the surface, while swallows and dragonflies work back and forth taking the insects as they emerge.

A few insects such as diving beetles and giant water bugs spend virtually all their lives in the water. The immature diving beetle larvae are known as water tigers, or dragons, and like the adults, they are fierce predators of tadpoles and even fish. The same is true of giant water bugs.

Both of these insect groups retain their wings and can fly to new ponds if necessary. It is not uncommon on a summer day to see insects raining out of the sky onto shiny automobiles. The insects flying far overhead apparently mistake the shine of the car for a pond's reflection and dive down onto the vehicle. I once experienced this in the middle of the Arizona desert. Diving beetles and giant water bugs sometimes fly at night and are likewise attracted to lights, making quite a commotion when they crash headlong into a lamp or a window.

There are many kinds of aquatic habitats. The surface supports its own distinctive fauna that depends on the phenomenon known as surface tension. Some aquatic beetles live on the underside of the surface film, crawling along upside down and plucking out insects trapped in the film. Water striders and whirligig beetles, two common aquatic insects, use the surface film as a feeding ground. Aided by sharp claws that allow it to grip the surface film and a water-repellent wax that coats the upper part of its feet, the water strider can run across the surface and even move upstream against the current.

Using the surface tension of the water, water striders stand up on their long, skinny legs and send out vibrations that travel along the surface. Because each leg has nerve sensors that can detect slight waves, water striders are able to communicate with one another in this way. To see this sensory system in action, catch a mosquito or other small insect and carefully toss it onto the surface of a pond. Sensing the vibration, water striders will skate across the water in the direction of the insect, which will often wind up impaled on the sharp proboscis of one of the water striders.

You can use the same trick with whirligig beetles. Swimming half in, half out of the water, the beetles take advantage of their habitat with rather unusual divided eyes, which enable them to see up out of the water as well as down into it at the same time. Like water striders, whirligig beetles feed on insects that get caught in the sur-

face film. But when you toss a larger object into the pond, the startled beetles react differently. They swim wildly around and around, turning and twisting in an effort to confuse a predator. When threatened, they may also dive beneath the water's surface.

The power of moving water has an important impact on aquatic insects. Large free-swimming insects are usually restricted to slow-moving or calm waters, where they are in no danger of being dragged away by the current.

Insects that thrive in fast-moving water have had to devise behaviours which protect them from being swept away. Stone flies, dobsonflies and mayflies often live under rocks or burrow into gravel, while blackflies attach themselves to river rocks with silk lines. Many caddis larvae build cases around their bodies, which they anchor to rocks with silk, using the current and the silk to snare food. Some species weave the finest mesh nets known, so intricate that they catch microscopic organisms too small for the human eye to see.

If you plan to add aquatic insects to your aquarium – or even to keep them in a large jar with a few waterweeds – it is best to use pond insects that do not require fast, clean, well-oxygenated water. Insects from cold streams are always difficult to maintain in captivity, and you should also remember that many of the large water beetles and bugs are capable of eating pet goldfish.

Social Insects

The worker honeybees coating the comb, above, have a variety of tasks, including ventilating the nest, gathering honey and pollen for the bee larvae, keeping the nest clean and defending the hive from predators. Army ant workers cooperate in capturing and transporting large prey, such as the wasp larva, right, that they are carrying through the Costa Rican rainforest.

Reaching down an old chipmunk burrow led to one of my most unpleasant surprises. A colony of yellow jackets had established an underground nest in the burrow. Angrily swarming out and up my sleeve, they stung me many times and chased me through the forest. My hand swelled up painfully until it looked like a pink balloon. That experience made me respect the vigorous defensive efforts of these highly social insects.

An ability to put up a strong defence is one of the advantages of living in a group. A hornets' nest is like a well-defended fortress, with many individuals ready to fight to protect the queen and other members of the social group living in the nest.

A social-insect colony is also much like a factory, whose purpose is to translate natural resources efficiently into an opportunity to raise offspring. Living in a group makes this task easier. Inside the hornets' nest, many individuals actively generate heat. The paperlike layers that make up the nest trap this warmth, and the adult wasps regulate the climate, keeping it relatively warm and well ventilated. On hot days, workers fan in fresh air at the nest entrance. In larger social-insect colonies, such as honeybee hives, a nearly constant temperature is maintained by the mass of bees and their ventilation activities.

The efficiency of the social-insect colony is the result of both the physical structures they build and the fact that social insects have a "division of labour." The main feature of this division of labour is that some insects in the colony reproduce and some perform other tasks. Such a strategy has developed in various types of bees, wasps, ants and termites and is best understood by studying the life cycle of a simple social-insect colony.

Consider a bumblebee colony. In spring, the hibernating queen emerges from the warming soil. Her first task is to feed, and she flies to newly opened willows, dandelions or white trilliums to collect nectar for energy and pollen for nutrients and vitamins. She then searches for a nest site — perhaps an abandoned vole nest in tall meadow grasses. There, she rearranges the nest insulation and begins to form a mass of wax, which she excretes from her body. Into this wax, she inserts her first clutch of eggs, which she sits on as a songbird would,

generating heat by shivering and contracting her muscles. When she runs out of energy and the day is warm, she flies off to collect more nectar to eat. If there is a surplus, she brings it back and stores it in wax pots that she constructs.

When the eggs hatch into larvae, the queen opens the wax pocket and slips in pollen that she has gathered from flowers and carried back in the tiny pollen baskets positioned on her hind legs. The larvae eat the pollen

and grow large. Within a few weeks, they hatch into adults. These bees are all females and are smaller than the queen. The new workers take over most of the work outside the nest. The queen normally remains protected in the nest, and her only duty is to lay and incubate eggs. The workers collect nectar and pollen. Some may specialize in guarding the nest entrance against mice, while others incubate eggs, feed larvae and ventilate the nest by fanning their wings.

As the end of summer approaches, the queen lays eggs that hatch into males and a set of large females, which will become next year's queens. The large females do little work; they simply feed and develop the store of fat they will need to hibernate over the winter. After mating outside the nest, they dig into the soil. All the other workers, the males and the old queen die with the arrival of snow.

This same system takes more elaborate forms. Honeybee colonies can

Like many social insects, termites, right, often have different worker types, or castes. The individuals with small, rounded heads are involved in gathering food and building the nests; those with large heads and pincerlike mouthparts are soldiers that attack intruders.

Leaf-cutting ants also produce a wide range of worker sizes, far right. Soldiers with massive heads defend the colonies, while medium-sized workers cut leaves for the mushroom culture the ants grow for food. The smallest workers tend the mushroom culture and also ride on the leaves, ready to attack any parasitic flies that approach the workers as they return to the colony with the vegetation.

overwinter, and the queen lives for several years. Some termite and ant queens may live for 10 years or more. These queens do nothing but lay eggs, and they resemble swollen sausages.

In the larger social-insect colonies, workers vary in size and have distinct duties. In leaf-cutting ant colonies, there are usually three types of workers. The soldiers, which have huge heads, defend the colony against attackers. Medium-sized workers do much of the leaf cutting, and the tini-

est workers either ride on the leaves that other workers carry to fend off the attacks of parasitic flies or remain in the nest tending the brood.

The leaf-cutting ant colony itself is equally well organized. There are chambers for growing fungi to feed the brood, chambers for laying new eggs and chambers for the maturing pupae. There is also a garbage pile for old debris and used-up fungi, and there are many ventilation shafts for air circulation.

The colony may include more than one million worker ants and extend dozens of metres underground. Leaf-cutting ants clear neat paths that run hundreds of metres through the forest to the selected trees they harvest. Scout ants communicate the location by laying down chemical trails. The workers then travel these paths to and from the food source. It is truly a complex society.

As we can see, social insects have a great capacity for learning, and that capacity is reflected in the size of their brains. The brain of a honeybee, for example, is 1/174 its body weight. By contrast, a water beetle's brain is only 1/4000 its weight. In relation to its body size, the honeybee's brain is more than 20 times as large as that of the water beetle. Clearly, an ability to live cooperatively calls for greater intelligence.

Elaborate and efficient communication about food or defence likewise becomes an important characteristic in the larger insect societies. Many social insects such as ants lay chemical trails, while honeybees use a special "waggle dance," whose choreography indicates the direction of the food. Other pheromones signal when a strong queen is present, and then only new workers will be raised. But when the queen's pheromone grows weaker as the queen ages, it triggers the production of new queens and males to replenish the colony.

Bees, ants and termites also release chemical alarm signals that indicate when the colony is under attack. Such signals mobilize other workers.

One very good reason to leave the area of a nest quickly if you are attacked and stung is that the sting gland itself releases an alarm-attack pheromone which will attract even more stinging workers.

The sting apparatus of members of the larger social-insect colonies such as honeybees is barbed, so it rips away from the bee's body after the bee stings an animal. Although this kills the bee, the sting gland keeps pumping poison into the animal. In other words, the detached sting apparatus continues to discourage the predatory animal from further attack. When a colony contains 50,000 or more workers, the death of a few is a small price to pay for saving the entire colony.

If the social insects lack a sting apparatus, as in the case of termites and many ants, a series of other equally effective weapons may be used. Some species have special soldiers with well-developed cutting jaws. Leaf-cutting ants have drawn blood when they have sliced into my finger. Termite soldiers act like chemical bombs. Their nozzle-shaped heads spray their attackers with a toxic, sticky secretion that smells like turpentine.

The best – and safest – way to learn about insect societies is to find an ant nest. Put out some sweet bait, such as honey, to attract ants, then follow them back to their nest. There, you can observe the ants in action. Watch them use their antennae to communicate with one another. Follow them to several food sources, and see what they eat and how they behave when they meet other ants and insects.

Symbiosis

In exchange for chasing off wasps and other predatory insects and thus helping to increase the survival rate of sap-sucking treehoppers, above, these ants receive a sugary secretion from the treehoppers. The relationship between ants and aphids, right, is also based on sugar given in return for protection. In some cases, ants may move aphids from plant to plant and even carry them underground for the winter.

If you were to open one of the huge nests of a colony of leaf-cutting ants found in the rainforests of Central and South America, you would discover much more than ants. Inside, you would find piles of greyish white fungi. These ants are, in fact, mushroom farmers.

Carving away sections of leaves, a food they are unable to digest, the leaf-cutting ants carry their harvest along trails that lead back to the nest. After chewing and cutting up the leaves, the ants add the greenery to the mushroom-growing piles. Because the ant nest has a well-regulated humid climate, it acts as a giant incubator for fungus culture. The fungi digest the plant material and produce small fruiting bodies that the ants find highly digestible.

By using the fungi, the ants are able to process large volumes of vegetation – one colony may consume as much as a cow does every day. Neither the ants nor the fungi can live without each other: the ants feed the fungi, and the fungi feed the ants.

Such biological partnerships are often useful because different individuals have complementary abilities. Insects have developed many living partnerships with other organisms that make use of the distinct biological abilities of each species. These close partnerships are examples of mutualism, or symbiosis – relationships in which both partners benefit.

Of all the insects, ants are most likely to have such partnerships, perhaps because they usually live in colonies with a fixed location and maintain a territory. This means that ants normally defend their partners, most of which provide food or shelter for the ants. As an example, ants often farm aphids – tiny insects that suck sap from plants – and protect them from parasites and predators. Ants will even carry aphids and their eggs underground in autumn to shield them from the killing frost of winter. When spring arrives, the ants carry the aphids back out and place them on plants, where they will be ready to begin another season's growth. If you find aphids in your garden, you will probably find ants standing guard over them. If you place another insect near the aphids, the ants will usually attack it and drive it away.

For their part, the aphids excrete rich honeydew that they tap from the plants with their long, tubular mouthparts. This honeydew provides the ants with a valuable source of energy that they cannot harvest themselves.

One of the most interesting and easy-to-find ant-aphid associations can be observed on alder trees, especially in late summer. Woolly alder aphids form dense, white, fluffy patches on the alders' stems. The aphids coat themselves with a waxy white excretion that may protect them somewhat from parasites, and they are usually tended by large, aggressive carpenter ants. However, a few predatory insects have successfully penetrated this defence. Among the patches of aphids, you may find the caterpillars of the harvester butterfly, one of the rare meat-eating caterpillars. By weaving a hidden

burrow that keeps it concealed from the ants, the caterpillar is able to sneak up, unseen by the ants, and feed on the aphids. After puncturing and consuming an aphid, the caterpillar uses the aphid skin as part of its burrow and so further conceals itself from the ants. Meanwhile, free-ranging ant lion larvae coat their backs with the aphids' white waxy fluff and likewise escape detection by the patrolling ants, even as they prey upon the aphids.

Some plants provide ants with nectar. Cherries, for example, ooze sweet sap from special glands on their twigs during spring to lure the ants that will keep the tree free from leaf-eating caterpillars. The plants that produce nectar on their foliage are quite numerous. In a garden, you can find elderberries, sunflowers, peonies and other common plants using sweet secretions to attract ants.

Several caterpillars have developed a mutualistic relationship with ants.

Hairstreak and metalmark butterfly caterpillars have special glands that excrete sugars and amino acids, the valuable building blocks that make up proteins. When they are approached by ants, the caterpillars produce a nutrient-rich droplet, in the same manner that aphids do. As a result, the ants then guard the caterpillars against predators. Without the ants, the caterpillars are eaten by spiders and predatory bugs and are attacked by parasitic wasps and flies.

Some types of acacia trees have evolved special structures to support acacia ant colonies, right. The orange bodies on the tips of new leaflets are used only to feed the ants. The trees also excrete nectar for ant food and have swollen hollow thorns that can be used for nest sites. In return, the ants, which are equipped with powerful stingers, attack caterpillars and deer and any other animals that try to eat the acacia leaves. The carpenter ant tending the hairstreak caterpillar, far right, draws a solution of amino acids and sugars from the caterpillar's dorsal gland.

This partnership is so highly developed that the caterpillars have evolved the ability to communicate with the ants by using sound vibrations which travel along the leaf's surface. The vibrations attract ants, which then begin to tend the caterpillars.

Some ant-plant partnerships are so strong that the ants live their entire lives within one kind of tree. Bull's horn acacia trees have large hollow thorns that are occupied by skinny, rust-coloured acacia ants. The trees produce not only nectar but also special oil- and protein-rich nodules on their young leaf tips. These provide all the nutrition the ant colony will ever need. To allow the tree better growing opportunities, the ants even trim away weeds from its base.

I once made the mistake of brushing against a bull's horn acacia tree in Costa Rica. Instantly, the ants swarmed over me, stinging and biting viciously. I left in a hurry, and I suspect that deer or other animals likewise avoid acacia trees and certainly do not regard them as a source of food.

A few insects carry their partners with them. The large dung beetles and carrion beetles that feed on decaying organic matter must sometimes compete with fly larvae for their food. Flies often arrive at the site first and lay many eggs, which quickly hatch into larvae that feed voraciously. Because the presence of these fly larvae will limit the beetle's ability to rear its own larvae, many of the beetles are aided by an army of mites that they carry with them. When the beetle arrives at the food source, the

mites swarm from the beetle, piercing and killing the fly eggs. By transporting the mites, the beetle reduces the competition for food. The mites benefit by being carried to an abundant food source by a powerful insect.

In some cases of mutualism, the symbiosis is invisible. Termites and cockroaches that eat wood and other hard-to-digest plant material are a good example. These insects can feed on woody debris because their guts are filled with tiny microorganisms that have special digestive enzymes which break down the woody material into useful nutrients. If termites were given an antibiotic that killed

these microbes, they would suffer from severe indigestion and would ultimately starve to death.

These protozoans are found only in association with termites and cockroaches and are the key to their biological success. In areas of Australia, South America and Africa, the savannas are dotted with mound after mound – some as high as three metres – each containing millions of termites that feed on the dry grass and dead wood produced every year. Such huge termite populations are able to thrive solely because of their invisible partnership with microscopically small organisms.

Pollination

Joe-pye weeds produce hundreds of small and easily accessible flowers which attract a wide variety of insects that feed on nectar, such as these swallowtail butterflies, above. The butterflies become coated with pollen and, as they move from plant to plant, fertilize other joe-pye-weed flowers. Bumblebees, right, not only move pollen from plant to plant but also collect the pollen and nectar as food for their larvae.

Always busy with bees, flies and beetles, a flower garden is an ideal place for observing insects. In fact, insects made the evolution of flowers possible. Magnolias, the earliest complex flowers to evolve, were first pollinated by beetles. Visiting the flowers for nectar, the beetles became coated with pollen. When they moved on to other magnolia flowers, the pollen rubbed off and fertilized the seeds.

Millions of years ago, before there were insects, plants had to depend on the wind to move their pollen from plant to plant, and as a result, much of the pollen was wasted. By carrying pollen directly from flower to flower, insects made pollination a far more efficient process. Gradually, many plants evolved flowers with nectar, colours or scents – all of which appeal to insect pollinators. Now, flowers are ingeniously designed for attracting specific kinds of insects.

Each type of flower draws different insect pollinators, and you can learn a lot about insects by studying flowers with a variety of shapes, colours and smells. Some flowers in the garden – dill, for instance – are not at all colourful or sweet-smelling. The tiny green flowers of dill attract equally tiny wasps and flies. By contrast, bright, sweet-smelling flowers like roses and sunflowers look the way they do in order to lure large bees.

Bumblebees are relatively strong, intelligent insects that have learned how to get inside complicated flowers like snapdragons, which keep away less effective pollinators such as flies. Attracted to blue, yellow and other bright colours, bees can even see the ultraviolet that is invisible to humans. As a result, the flower we look at may appear quite different to a bee. Complicated bee flowers like violets and snapdragons often have "nectar guides" – conspicuous lines of colour that point the way toward the flower opening and the nectar.

Most insects, including bees, do not see red and are therefore less attracted to this colour than to others. Study the insects that visit white trilliums and red trilliums, and you will notice that bumblebees are attracted only to the white trilliums. Small flies are drawn to red trilliums, but more because of their mouldy smell than their colour.

Butterflies, on the other hand, do see red, and butterfly flowers, such as many milkweeds, are orange-red.

They are even designed with a platformlike structure that makes landing easy for the nectar-hungry butterflies. You can attract large numbers of butterflies to your garden by planting these kinds of flowers.

By contrast, flowers such as jasmine that cater to night-flying moths are usually white and give off a powerful sweet scent only in the evening. I have tried growing some of the large desert nightshade plants in my house, but it smelled as though I had spilled a bottle of perfume. The scent was just too overpowering. Both their strong odour and white colour make these flowers easy for insects to find at night, and the large sphinx moth, which looks not unlike a hummingbird in the dim light of night, dives right inside the flower to drink the pool of sweet nectar at its base.

Not all flowers smell sweet, though, and not all insects like sugar. There are flowers on thorny green brier vines and large tropical lilies that do not smell nice at all. In fact, the largest flower in the world, the *Raffelesia* vine of the Indonesian rainforest, is as wide as a bicycle wheel and simply reeks. The flowers smell of decaying meat, and you can probably guess what swarms around them: flies and beetles that feed on carrion. By mimicking the scent of decay, these flowers attract a special set of pollinators.

It is to every plant's advantage to make itself appealing to its pollinators, and some plants have devised

however, and not all flowers provide insects with compensation for their efforts. A few simply deceive and trap them. Pink and yellow lady's-slipper orchids use colour and scent to draw bees into their hollow slipper-shaped flowers. Once inside, the bee discovers that there is no nectar to be had. Eventually, as it tries to escape by squeezing through a tight opening that is the flower's only exit, its back is smeared with orchid pollen. If it falls for the same trick twice and visits another lady's-slipper, the second flower will then be pollinated. Instead of receiving food for its role in the pollination process, the bee has been manipulated by the flower. But this is a rare phenomenon. Most flowers reward the insects that visit them with either nectar or pollen.

Flowers attract more than just pollinators. Predictably, they also draw the predators of pollinators. When you're walking through a field, take a closer look at summer daisies and black-eyed Susans, and you will often see crab spiders lurking there, camouflaged on the petals, ready to bite, paralyze and digest the insects that come seeking nectar and pollen.

The complicated structures of flowers combined with the huge variety of insects mean that pollination is a highly complex and fascinating event. A garden, a field or a forest filled with flowers can become a ready-made guessing game, in which you try to determine which kinds of insects will be attracted to which kinds of flowers. To discover the answers, all you have to do is wait and watch.

unusual behaviours for this purpose. Night-flowering philodendrons heat up to more than 38 degrees C in order to attract scarab beetles. Eastern skunk cabbages (northern relatives of philodendrons) flower when there is still snow on the ground. Their heat melts away the snow and sends off the skunky smell needed to draw the first flies of the season.

If you keep an eye on giant sunflowers over the course of the day, you will find that they move. Slowly but surely, the flowers rotate so that they always face the sun. That makes them attractive to insects which require the warmth of the sun to stay active. The big flowers are visited by a wide range of insects, including bees, flies, wasps and beetles.

There are exceptions to every rule,

Insects like the sulphur butterfly, above right, are powerful fliers that need an abundance of sugar. In this way, the pollen of nectar-producing flowers that attract butterflies is transferred to plants several kilometres away. Insect predators sometimes take advantage of the pollination phenomenon. Camouflaged against the white petals of a daisy, this crab spider, far right, has ambushed a timothy skipper looking for nectar.

Communication

Tropical stingless bees arriving at the nest entrance, above, communicate the location of food sources to one another by laying a trail of chemical scent marks. Male luna moths have much larger antennae than do females, right. The antennae are used by males to detect and follow scent trails released by females ready to mate.

One of the most mysteriously beautiful sights of summer is an evening meadow twinkling with fireflies. The soft green lights appear and disappear and move through the night. If you pursue one of these blinking lights and gently sweep it out of the air with a net or your hand, you will find that the light comes not from a fly but from a soft brownish or grey beetle.

The light generated chemically in the firefly's body is a communication system. The blinking action signals whether the beetle is male or female, and by varying the rate and the pattern of blinking in a kind of Morse code, different types of fireflies can indicate their exact identity. Light flashing, which is simply an exchange of information between individuals, need not be a conscious act. The only requirement is that a signal is sent by one insect and received by another.

Because insects rely heavily on chemical communication, most of their signals are invisible to us. Silk moths, for example, use chemical communication to attract mates. A friend of mine used to study silk moths. To find males, he would put a female silk moth in a small cage and hang the cage outside at dusk. Within a few hours, a small cloud of male silk moths would be flying around the cage. The female produces a chemical signal known as a pheromone. While this pheromone cannot be detected by humans, male silk moths can "smell" it several kilometres away and follow it to the source. When you see silk moths clustered around a light, you will notice the huge feathery antennae of the males. The antennae help the moths to decipher the chemical communications.

Insect pheromones are widely used, and you can sometimes see them in action. If you examine the moths around a light at night, you may see a small silvery moth known as a pyralid slowly waving the tail end of its abdomen while displaying a plume of scales. These are scent scales, and they emit a pheromone to attract other pyralids for mating.

Since scientists began to understand them, pheromones have become important tools for pest control. Using pheromones to produce chemicals that mimic the lure, biologists can bait traps to attract pest moths, such as the male gypsy moth, or can soak a field with so much pheromone that the insects become confused and are unable to reproduce effectively.

Not all chemical signals are airborne. Social insects rub pheromones on the ground or on vegetation as chemical trails to communicate the presence and direction of food. To observe this behaviour, put out some bait for ants – a bit of sugar water, for instance – then watch the first ants to discover the bait. After drinking their fill, they hurry back to the nest, dragging their abdomens along the ground. This is called laying a trail. The next ants to arrive run along this invisible trail, smelling the chemical with their antennae and heading straight to the food. As more and more ants make the trip, the trail becomes stronger, and the ants run rapidly to and from the food source.

You can conduct a simple experiment to show how this trail works. Place the bait on a piece of plywood on the ground and allow the ants to discover it and to establish a foraging trail. Then carefully rotate the plywood 180 degrees. The ants, in a state of confusion, will go in the wrong direction, away from their nests.

Tent caterpillars use a line of silk to communicate the direction of their feeding ground. Watch as the caterpillars leave the tent in the morning, and you will see that they follow silk trails which lead to feeding sites. When the leaves on one limb are finished, the caterpillars will move to other branches, but as they do, they will lay down a thread of silk to mark their return route.

Sometimes, a pheromone communicates a "stay away" message. Parasitic wasps often mark their hosts with a chemical signature that discourages other wasps from parasitizing the insect egg or caterpillar. If too many eggs were laid in the same host, the larvae would starve.

Insects also rely heavily on sound for communication. If a tuning fork is struck outside in summer, it will often attract male mosquitoes, which mistake the sound for that of a female. Chirping crickets sing by rubbing their wing files together. Male grasshoppers and katydids produce an amazing array of sounds with their wing or leg files. The signals are used to court females or to repel males. But other species are able to eavesdrop on such communications. Certain parasitic flies follow cricket chirps to find crickets that they will use as food for their larvae. When a recording of cricket calls is played, these flies buzz around the loudspeakers. Cats have been observed hunting crickets by listening to their calls. Biting midges home in on the courtship calls of tree frogs and then take a blood meal.

If they are accidentally buried, ants will emit a high-pitched squeak to attract other ants to come to their rescue. Ants depend on touch as well. Watch closely the next time you see two ants meet on a trail. The workers touch by drumming their antennae on each other's head. After this communication, food is often exchanged. If you take an ant from its own colony or an area some distance away and place it near another ant colony, you will see a completely different reaction. When two unrelated ants meet, they either run away from each other or fight. Their scent and touch are enough to communicate that they are rivals rather than nestmates.

Pests and Pesticides

Tent caterpillars sunning on the outside of their silken nest, above, thrive in disturbed habitats where there are introduced plants, such as apple trees, and fewer natural predators and parasites. Habitats untouched by humans usually have far fewer pest-insect outbreaks. Because agricultural crops attract parasites and pests that multiply rapidly, farmers often resort to spraying pesticides, right, which then frequently pollute nearby water sources.

To people who are afraid of insects, almost any insect is a pest. But a more useful definition of an insect pest is a species that interferes with the activities of people. Most insect pests are either bloodsucking insects, especially those which transmit diseases, or agricultural pests, which eat crops or attack livestock. Although repulsive to many of us, insects that thrive in human housing, like cockroaches, are more of a cosmetic concern. They do not cause negative health effects, and in fact, we could say they even have a benefit: they provide employment for pest exterminators.

Insect pests have played a huge role in human history. Epidemics such as the bubonic plague, or the Black Death, which killed millions of Europeans during the Middle Ages, were caused by microorganisms transmitted by flea bites. Insects such as fleas, which have direct contact with the bloodstream, pose the greatest risk for humans. They open a pathway for organisms to spread quickly throughout our bodies.

Insect-spread diseases are still a very real problem for humans, despite the scientific advances we have made. Yellow fever, dengue and encephalitis epidemics spread by mosquitoes have killed millions of people in South America and Africa. Malaria, a blood parasite carried by mosquitoes, still infects 200 million people around the world. Chagas' disease is another blood parasite spread by a bug that lives in South America. Tropical sand flies transmit leishmaniasis, a microorganism that destroys tissue.

Insects also cause massive crop losses around the world. In the past, outbreaks of insects have resulted in devastating famines. Locusts have long been a problem, and more specific pests have destroyed crops that are grown on a large scale, such as rice and wheat.

Many of the worst pests are also the most difficult to control. Among them are those which thrive in unnatural environments or have been transplanted to new environments where they flourish. Malaria, for example, is the biggest problem in the squalid, dirty cities of the Tropics, where poor sanitation and drainage provide ample breeding sites for pest mosquitoes and where human poverty does not allow for good health care. In an untouched rainforest, though, malaria is not a significant danger, because there are relatively few mosquitoes and few humans, both of which are needed to pass on the disease.

It is in human-created agricultural environments that pest outbreaks become explosively large and persistent. Consider the mustard butterfly caterpillar, which first fed on weedy mustard plants along riverbanks and in small clearings in the original forests that once covered Europe. The caterpillar was attacked by many parasites and predators, including all sorts of birds and insects that lived in the forests. The caterpillar's food plants were mixed among dozens of inedible species, and as a result, the caterpillar rarely became superabundant. But when the forests were cut and burned and turned into fields, many of the

predator and parasite populations were eliminated. Great stretches of mustard-family plants such as cabbages were grown by farmers, and all of these crop plants were highly edible to the mustard butterfly caterpillar. It is not surprising, then, that the butterfly multiplied hugely and became a pest of human agriculture.

Now, imagine accidentally importing the mustard butterfly to North America, where it had never lived before and there are no native parasites adapted to attack the caterpillar. Instead, there is an abundance of cabbage, mustard, broccoli and other food plants. The result: This once rare European butterfly has become a difficult pest that can be found in almost every garden in North America.

There are many such examples.

Gypsy moths are another pest that was inadvertently introduced to North America from Europe and has spread widely, destroying millions of hectares of forest. The bristly caterpillars have almost no parasites to deal with, and few North American birds will eat them. As a result, humans have had to resort to other control measures.

Over the past 40 years, we have increasingly come to rely on toxic chemicals to control insect pests as more farmland is created, more pests are spread and there are fewer natural enemies, such as birds and parasites. Poison sprays are applied to crops and to the soil to kill insect pests quickly and inexpensively. But the ecological costs of such methods are high.

DDT, for example, was once a popular pesticide in North America. Now, it is banned here, although our governments do nothing to prevent North American companies from manufacturing and shipping it to underdeveloped countries. The environmental problem that DDT causes is related to its effectiveness: it and its chemical relatives are slow to break down in nature. When DDT enters an ecosystem, it stays there, spreading through waterways and poisoning wildlife. Even distant areas of the oceans are now contaminated with DDT and other pesticide runoff. The pesticides accumulate in the tissues of animals such as eagles, whales and humans, causing severe health problems. Several bird species have nearly become extinct because of pesticides.

Insects eventually develop a re-

sistance to widely used pesticides, so new ones have to be continually invented and applied. Our environment is therefore gradually accumulating more and more kinds of pesticides, whose impact on wildlife, water and people is poorly understood.

In some cases, pesticides that degrade quickly or poisons that are more selective have been developed. Gypsy moth outbreaks are sprayed with *Bacillus thuringiensis*, commonly known as Bt, a bacterium that infects caterpillars and causes them to die. While this method is clearly better than spraying with DDT, gypsy moths are just one kind of caterpillar. A forest is home to hundreds of the caterpillars of other nonpest moths and butterflies, many of which are both beautiful and necessary. They provide the food for forest birds. What happens to the forest birds when Bt is sprayed, causing a massive die-off of caterpillars? Nobody really knows.

The best approach to pest control is for humans to try to reestablish the biological checks – parasites and predators – that once kept pest populations at a reasonable level. An option for farmers is to introduce parasites into their fields and to grow pest-resistant plant varieties. Planting smaller fields with a greater diversity of crops, rather than just one plant type, also limits pest outbreaks. Such methods are time-consuming and cost money. Food produced in this way is more expensive. But the price we will ultimately pay for polluting our planet and destroying its biological diversity is far, far higher.

Credits

The Architecture of Animals: The Equinox Guide to Wildlife Structures
Adrian Forsyth
Camden House, 1989

The Audubon Society Field Guide to North American Insects and Spiders
Lorus Milne and Margery Milne
Alfred A. Knopf, 1980

How Nature Works
David Burnie
Reader's Digest, 1991

Insects
Ross E. Hutchins
Prentice-Hall, 1966

A Practical Guide for the Amateur Naturalist
Gerald Durrell
Alfred A. Knopf, 1989

Further Reading

Index